independence:
building upon the strengths of aging people

Independence:
BUILDING UPON THE
STRENGTHS OF AGING PEOPLE

Frances Taira, *RNC, MSN, Ed.D.*

Assistant Professor of Nursing
Loyola University of Chicago

TECHNOMIC
PUBLISHING CO., INC.

LANCASTER · BASEL

Randall Library UNC-W

Published in the Western Hemisphere by
Technomic Publishing Company, Inc.
851 New Holland Avenue
Box 3535
Lancaster, Pennsylvania 17604 U.S.A.

Distributed in the Rest of the World by
Technomic Publishing AG

© 1988 by Technomic Publishing Company, Inc.
All rights reserved

No part of this publication may be reproduced, stored in a
retrieval system, or transmitted, in any form or by any means,
electronic, mechanical, photocopying, recording, or otherwise,
without the prior written permission of the publisher.

Printed in the United States of America
10 9 8 7 6 5 4 3 2 1

Main entry under title:
  Independence: Building Upon the Strengths of Aging People

A Technomic Publishing Company book
Bibliography: p.
Includes index p. 183

Library of Congress Card No. 88-50177
ISBN No. 87762-549-2

RA
777.6
.T33
1988

Acknowledgement   ix

PART I: *Promoting Independence and Healthy Aging*

Chapter 1: How to Promote Independence   3

The Need for Family Assistance 4
Developmental Tasks of Later Maturity 5
How Community Agencies Promote Independence 8

Chapter 2: Adapting to Physical Changes   14

Adaptation to Change 15
Lack of Oxygen 15
Body Temperature Problems 15
Impaired Metabolism 16
Immobility 17
Reduced Vision 18
Vision and Driving Tips from the American 19
    Optometric Association
Resources for the Blind 20
Reduced Hearing 21
The Family and Physical Changes 23

Chapter 3: Preventing Chronic Illness   25

Causes of Chronic Illness 25
Levels of Prevention 26
Accident Prevention 32

Chapter 4: Exercise   37

Benefits of Exercise 37
Exercise Programs 39

Chapter 5: Nutrition and Aging   44

Adequate Nutrition 45
U.S. Dietary Goals 46
Food Budget 47
Meals on Wheels 48
Obesity 51
Tips on Dieting 52

Chapter 6: Financial Planning for Health Care   55

Developing a Budget 56
Obtaining Financial Assistance 58
Finding Employment 62

Chapter 7: Adapting to Psychosocial Changes   70

Theories of Psychological Aging 71
Depression 72
Sexuality 73
Promoting Mental Health 74

Chapter 8: Stress   77

Reactions to Stress 77
Stress and Disease 79

Chapter 9: The Arts and Aging   85

Objectives of an Arts Program 86
The Theater 86
Recordings for Recovery 88
Literature 88
Family Participation 91

Chapter 10: Legal and Ethical Concerns   92

An Elderly Legal Services Program 93
Estate Planning Checklist 94
Consumer Fraud 96
Family Friends 96
The Friend/Advocate 98
Ethics and the Volunteer Guardian 100

Chapter 11: Shelter   103

Homesharing 106
Nursing Home Projects 108
Accessory Apartments 111
Energy Conservation 112
Home Equity 112

PART II: *Maintaining Independence in People with Health Problems*

Chapter 12: Nursing Care and Maintaining Function   117

Observations 119
Activities of Daily Living 121
Basic Skills 123
Maintaining Function 124

Chapter 13: Long-Term Use of Medication   128

Physiological Changes and Drugs 128
Drug Education 130
Use of Media 135
The Quack 136

Chapter 14: Cardiovascular and Respiratory Problems   140

Peripheral Vascular Disease 140
Angina 141
Congestive Heart Failure 141
Stroke 142
Chronic Obstructive Pulmonary Disease 145
Pneumonia 146

Chapter 15: Cancer   148

Warning Signs 149
Treatment 149
Sites of Cancer 152

Chapter 16: Common Chronic Health Problems   155

Recurring Fractures 156
Arthritis 157
Diabetes 158
Gastrointestinal Problems 160
Urinary Tract Problems 161

Chapter 17: Loss of Intellect   163

Acute Organic Brain Syndrome 163
Alzheimer's Disease 164
Rehabilitation 165
Abuse of the Aged 166

Chapter 18: Elderly Volunteers   167

Helping People in Detention 167
Intergenerational Projects 169

Chapter 19: Obtaining Assistance from Others   173

Home Health Agencies 174
Senior Centers 176
The Independents 177
Doctors 178
Support Groups 179

Chapter 20: In Conclusion   181

Index   183

This book was born out of my observation in working with elderly clients that they desired as much independence as possible. I am grateful to my colleagues nationwide for sharing with me case studies and background material from their files.

FRANCES TAIRA

promoting independence and healthy aging

how to promote independence

This book offers suggestions to families on how to promote independence in their elderly relatives. The first section of the book deals with independence and healthy aging. It discusses how people can:

- adapt to the physiological and psychosocial changes of aging
- handle stress
- prevent chronic illness
- maintain a healthy lifestyle

The second section of the book deals with independence and people with health problems. It discusses how people can:

- understand and cope with common chronic health problems
- obtain assistance when necessary

In addition to being helpful to elderly people and their families, this book will also be helpful to community leaders. It provides examples and case studies from community agencies throughout the United States, explaining how they have solved problems related to maintaining independence in the elderly.

When I teach nursing care of the elderly to nursing students, I tell them, "Look for strengths. Don't focus on weaknesses." During clinical teaching, I arrange for my students to visit the elderly in their own homes. These students are often amazed to see how the elderly can maintain an independent living style, even if they have to manage chronic health problems. As Tom Romano, Executive Director of the East Shore Regional Adult Daycare Center in Connecticut, wrote to me, "In my opinion there is nothing magical or mystical about caring for the frail elderly and disabled adult. I believe all or most of us are born with a natural instinct to become independent. Through common sense, communication, co-operation, initiative, innovativeness and shared resources (networking), we can all assist each other in attaining or maintaining an enhanced quality of life."

The Need for Family Assistance

In spite of the instinct to become independent, there will be times when the elderly need help from their families. A decrease in the mortality of the very old will lead to an increase in the number of frail elderly. The U.S. Bureau of the Census projects that by the year 2000 we will have 14.4 million people over seventy-five years of age. From 1990 to 2000 there will be an increase of 31 percent, to 3.8 million, in the number of people over eighty-five years of age.

The more dependent a person has become, the more time and money it will take to help him to become independent. The majority of elderly people are currently independent. They need to know how to reduce the risk of illness, by following the principles of good nutrition and exercise, and by learning to handle stress. These measures are less costly than rehabilitating a dependent elderly person, where there is a need to adapt the home environment and to buy walking aids, etc.

Home nursing care is preferable to institutionalization. People get well faster in the comfort of their own home. A patient told me today that it was impossible to rest adequately in a hospital with so much noise, day and night. People walk by talking; I.V. machines beep; and confused patients cry out. This complaint is not unusual.

The costs of care are less at home. Medicare or private insurance may pay for part of the care of a home health nurse, who will teach the patient and family how to cope at home. Even people very competent in their own occupations need this teaching in home nursing, so that they know what to do and how to do it.

This book is intended to help family members to prevent illness and, when necessary, to care for a sick elderly person at home. It provides basic information about a variety of health problems, to increase understanding of the causes of these problems and potential treatments. This understanding will enable family members to improve their ability to give care. The information is presented in clear, simple language.

Part I (Chapters 1–11) focuses on prevention of illness as it applies to the elderly. The normal physical and psychosocial changes in aging may predispose the person to illness, unless appropriate preventive measures are taken. Part II (Chapters 12–20) focuses on maintaining independence while coping with common physical or psychosocial health problems. It is necessary to consider a person's chronic health problems and treatment plan when trying to solve current acute health problems. What if an elderly person who has chronic heart problems twists an ankle? A person expends a lot of energy walking on crutches. The potential treatment for the twisted ankle may have to be adjusted to allow for the activity limitations necessitated by the chronic health problem.

This book will help you to make a realistic assessment of your strengths and of your elderly family member's strengths. At the end of each chapter, readers are given suggestions on how to apply what they have learned. The emphasis of the book is on this practical application of information.

Developmental Tasks of Later Maturity

One thinks of learning new tasks as a job for the young, but elderly people also have to learn new ways of behaving as they age. Robert Havighurst, a professor at the University of Chicago, perceived that older adults had certain developmental tasks to achieve. Successful achievement of these tasks led to happiness, whereas failure to achieve the tasks led to unhappiness. Is your elderly relative struggling to achieve any of these six developmental tasks as delineated by Havighurst?

1. Adjusting to Decreasing Physical Strength and Health

Aging leads to a loss of functions of cells. There are various theories of why this happens. One theory suggests that there is a program built into the genes which determines a person's life span, given optimal circumstances. Environmental trauma reduces this potential by causing the cell function to become diminished, or by killing the cell. Another theory suggests that aging cells are less efficient in eliminating waste products, which allows these products to build up and poison the cell.

The aging immune system is less effective in destroying mutated cells. As the number of mutated cells increases, this leaves fewer normal cells in the organ to adequately carry out its desired function. The aging immune system may even participate in an autoimmune reaction, attacking the body's own normal cells as if they were mutations. This can lead to arthritis and other diseases. A healthy lifestyle can do much to prevent disease, and enable a person to live as long as his potential life span.

2. Adjustment to Retirement and Reduced Income

A job provides income and companionship. Retirement liberates the person from a daily routine, but sometimes the retired person has not prepared himself to use all the leisure time he now has. People may plan more for a two week vacation than they plan for twenty years of retirement living. Many companies are now offering pre-retirement programs to assist workers to set goals for their retirement. Such programs are more beneficial if offered at least five years before the planned retirement date.

A person who realizes that with inflation he will have difficulty maintaining his lifestyle after retirement may decide to keep on working. If he is able to postpone retirement, then he has a longer time to build up savings for retirement. It may be difficult to maintain close relationships with friends from work if decreased income curtails participation in social events. Social contacts are needed to replace lost relationships with former colleagues.

3. Adjustment to Death of Spouse

A widower will probably have to learn how to cook and care for himself, but his chances for remarriage are good. A widow has fewer opportunities for remarriage, since there are more older women than older men, and society is more accepting of older men marrying younger women than of older women marrying younger men. Both widows and widowers have to cope with the grief of losing a loving companion. In addition to this loneliness, a widow may find herself poor as retirement benefits are cut in half when her husband dies—particularly if she has not worked long enough to accumulate her own benefits. A federal government worker who does not choose to take a reduction in his retirement annuity to provide for his widow now has to present a signed document from his wife agreeing to waive her rights. If this policy continues in force, it is a move in the right direction to protect widows from destitution.

Today's young women smoke and work outside the home in stressful occupations, which leaves them more at risk for chronic diseases. Perhaps, because of these factors, in future years women will no longer outlive their spouses. Of course, the longer women work outside the home, the more independent they will be in relation to planning for their own retirement.

4. Establishing an Explicit Affiliation with One's Age Group

The elderly become physically tired more easily than the young. Therefore, they can have difficulty in keeping up with the middle-aged group. Also, they have less income to spend. If people choose to become involved in one of the many organizations whose membership is predominately elderly, then they have many opportunities for friendships and shared interests.

I can appreciate that after I retire from nursing I will probably reduce my participation in the nursing research organization I belong to and increase my participation in the American Association of Retired Persons, just as I joined the PTA when my children were of school age and left the PTA when my children graduated. However, I am philosophically committed to intergenerational co-operation and would hope that task number 4 would not be used as a rationale for relegating elders to socializing only with their own age group.

5. Meeting Social and Civic Obligations

As the percentage of the population which is elderly increases, the elderly are acquiring more power to impact on elections. There is a need for all citizens to be knowledgeable about political issues, so they can vote wisely.

6. Establishing Satisfactory Physical Living Arrangements

There are many different shelter options for the elderly:

- Remain in one's own home with assistance as necessary.
- Move to a smaller house or an apartment.
- Live in a retirement community.
- Move into a nursing home.

In choosing among these options, the elderly person has to consider his level of income, health, and available family support.

How Community Agencies Promote Independence

Rhonna Burrelle, the Program Manager for the Aleutian-Pribilof Islands Association in Alaska, enlightened me about the importance of taking into account the history of long-term dependence in Alaska, when promoting independence. She stated:

> The notion of independence among the aged in this region is at the very first steps on a ladder of what might be a long range of independence. Because of a history which involved ancestral domination by Russians, followed by a very strict colonized and autocratic control by American administrators and officials, the aged are particularly passive and dependent. For purposes of illustration, older adults in San Francisco are accustomed to shopping, doing things for themselves, performing simple home maintenance, and thus have a history of self-management in areas other than health care. In contrast, consider a community in this region whose elderly comprise a generation taken care of by those in power—the government structure—and were forced to be fairly passive in terms of their own activity. When a door latch was broken, a government worker was dispatched to repair it. To this day, there is no hardware, nails or lumber sold in the store or available on the island. Therefore, while it is commonly accepted that most Americans are passive consumers of medical services, the notion of promoting independence is much more elementary among the aged in this region—a generation which has a history of very little self-management.
>
> Workshops were held to identify and refine activities which would promote health, were understandable, and would be used by older adults. These activity-oriented sessions were conducted in such a way that participants—who knew each other and had frequent contact with one another—reinforced their own mastery through helping others, and through group recognition of what they were doing. The promotion of self-care among the aged is a long-term process, and not something that can be done in one month or one year. The program must be administered in such a way that it is community-based and needs to perpetuate and continue itself rather than be constantly provided for by a central agency located miles and miles away. A self-perpetuating, continuing program involves a multigenerational approach—both in terms of the promotion of self-care (the desired outcome) and administration.
>
> Most approaches that target the elderly presuppose that the aged are a legitimate, definable subset of a larger community. Each of the eleven communities in this region are isolated and separate from one another. These communities are then, by nature, interdependent. One consequence is increased interaction among and between all ages. In fact, there is probably more multigenerational interaction than there is within generation interaction, simply because of the size of the communities (keep in mind these communities are very small, as are the numbers of

those over sixty). Older adults interact with people that are younger more often than with each other because of extended family traditions, living conditions, and the nature of life in small, rural native communities.

Cross-age cadres are being trained to provide on-going training activities for older adults. Some of these individuals, as well as their peers, suffer—to a larger degree than would be expected—from the same health problems as the older population. Those who are learning the techniques of self-care to teach the aged are learning by teaching, and as a consequence become more capable and willing to use self-care activities for themselves as a secondary outcome of promoting self-care among the elderly. The program may serve to potentiate younger generations and in effect, preempt the need for training self-managing skills to these generations when they are older.

In Alaska the different generations lived in one community. What can you do to help an elderly relative if she lives in Florida or California and refuses to move, whereas you live in New York? You cannot afford to keep flying back and forth. You need to investigate what resources are available for this elderly person in her current living situation, if she chooses to go on living alone.

Harry Schumacher, a Florida Regional Administrator, disclosed that:

> The older people of Sarasota County know that they can call on Senior Friendship Centers when they need help. The services that Senior Friendship Centers provide to persons sixty and over are geared to offset the isolation and loneliness that so frequently characterize the lives of the elderly. Our motto is PEOPLE HELPING PEOPLE and that is more than just a catchy slogan with us for we see it being lived out every day in the lives of those people. By providing opportunities for interaction we help them to avoid the depression which is the most common illness among the elderly.
>
> Our organization operates on a continuum of service principle so that we consider not so much the age factor but the person's level of need. What is this person's need at this particular time? We try to meet whatever need an older person has, and if that need is not among the services we provide then we put that person in touch with some other organization or agency that will meet that need.
>
> One of the services that we offer which specifically assists in maintaining independence is our homemaker service. Sometimes because of frailty or a debilitating illness an older person is no longer able to keep up the home or apartment. The relatives up north may be insisting that the older person move into a retirement home or move in with them. Our homemaker service will send someone into the home to tidy up, wash the windows, clean the bathroom, change the bed linens, do the

laundry and the shopping, etc. Then when the relatives learn that Senior Friendship Center is providing this support system they stop "nagging" the older person since that person is thus able to retain their independence.

Our adult day care center is another service that enables the frail elderly to avoid being institutionalized when they do not need institutional care. It relieves the children of the concern for those elders while the family is off at work or school all day.

Our health service is staffed by thirty-one volunteer physicians, twenty-eight retired nurses, and office personnel. Because they volunteer their services, the elderly who are not so poor that they qualify for the public health department nor so well off that they can afford private medical care in Sarasota, are able to see a physician on a regular basis without worrying about bills. Once again it is PEOPLE HELPING PEOPLE, for not only are these retired medical personnel helping these older people, but it is also helping the medical personnel to stay in touch with their lifetime profession. As one retired doctor said, "You can do only so much fishing, so much playing golf."

The Senior Community Centers of San Diego have as their Director of Community Development Chris Wagner, who described a special program:

> Hotel Alert is a flexible and responsive program that assists older persons to maintain their independent and self-reliant lifestyle in the community. It can be tailored to any urban area in the country. The critical element is community support—which we are fortunate to have in downtown San Diego.

Chris refers to his clients as the "downtown elderly." He continued:

> When the agency opened its second center to serve a growing older population in the area south of Broadway in 1978, we came into contact with an isolated group of seniors—low income elderly residing in single room occupancy (SRO) hotels. Predominantly male and poor, they have led mobile and non-traditional lives. They seldom marry, produce few children, and are unlikely to be in close contact with any children they father. They value independence and self-reliance, typically have few people in their social networks, and tend to rely heavily upon the informal or "natural helping network" of hotel managers, desk clerks, storekeepers and other residents to meet their daily needs.
>
> It is important to note that the SRO lifestyle exists in urban areas throughout the United States—it is not special to San Diego. Research has shown that the elderly living in SROs are a unique population, surviving, in the words of author Margaret Clark, "by their wits." The decision to live in the downtown area is one of choice. The desire of this group to remain independent and to provide for their own needs despite

physical and economic hardship makes the SRO hotel and its support a logical alternative to more structured institutions.

Although most SRO residents choose to handle their own problems, hotel staff are important. Desk clerks and managers "keep an eye" on older residents, screen visitors, offer credit, make loans and give advice. Other caretakers (shopkeepers, waitresses, post office clerks, police) offer a structure for social relationships. The downtown area offers a variety of services (cheap restaurants offering balanced diets, second-hand clothing stores, discount drug stores, hotels with laundromats, nearby police and affordable public transportation). For the older resident existing on an income of less than $450 a month (Social Security), the availability of such goods and services allows them to remain independent.

Many of the bureaucratized social/health agencies are viewed negatively and avoided whenever possible. Older residents view health-oriented caretakers as being primarily interested in the "medicine buck" and not their well-being. Similarly, social service agencies are viewed as a threat and not frequented. However, the SRO residents' desire to remain independent and self-reliant at all costs can often work against them. Their avoidance of community agencies and services contributes to their vulnerability in times of crisis. With appropriate assistance, many older persons are able to continue to live within their apartments. The alternative is often abandonment to expensive care in custodial institutions.

Recognizing the inability of traditional social services to reach the single room occupant, two social work interns from San Diego State University developed an outreach program to locate and assist downtown SRO residents. This effort, known as Hotel Alert, was designed to link a social worker with the existing natural helpers (staff and other residents) in the SROs. The social worker trained the managers and other hotel staff in the types of problems and concerns facing elderly residents, services available within the downtown area and how to effectively utilize them. A directory of agencies, categorized by area of concern, was provided to hotel managers. In addition to hotel staff, local law enforcement officers assigned to the downtown were involved in the program to enlist their aid in referring seniors in need of services. Hotel staff, senior residents and the police were all provided with a Hotel Alert card to call us directly or refer seniors.

Today, thirty-five hotels participate in the Hotel Alert program. Regular contacts are made with each hotel twice monthly. Hotel staff and residents are provided with agency newsletters, updated listings of downtown service agencies and other appropriate resources. Information is collected about the specific needs of downtown residents, and meetings are regularly held with hotel managers. The Hotel Alert worker also contacts community agencies and makes listings of downtown hotels available as an emergency housing resource. The program is widely known and utilized by hospitals, downtown social service agencies and medical facilities. Other community people are involved in efforts to locate seniors in need—Bar Alert distributes weekly menus for the congregate meal program at our Center to nineteen local bars. A stepchild of Hotel Alert, this service encourages bartenders to be alert for older persons with nutrition, companionship and social service needs.

The Hotel Alert worker's role is that of a "generalist"—to provide whatever types of assistance the situation may call for. Upon referral of an elderly person requiring aid, the worker applies appropriate intervention strategies (crisis intervention, counseling, help locating emergency food, medical and personal assistance, general information, transportation, etc.). The worker serves as a case manager to locate and obtain other services that may be needed.

Because of the variety of programs available through Senior Community Centers, the Hotel Alert worker can provide comprehensive assistance to an older person residing within the downtown area. The South Center is located within a ten block radius of most of the hotels, allowing easy access on foot or by bus. Congregate meals are offered five days a week, and meals are delivered to homebound elderly unable to prepare their own food or leave their home. Through the close relationship with Mercy Hospital and San Diego Square Senior Center, a nurse practitioner offers free health screenings and assessments, and is available to accompany the Hotel Alert worker to visit SRO residents unwilling or unable to use medical facilities.

One of the unique qualities of the Hotel Alert program is its ability to follow up on seniors who have received services. Because of the independent nature of the SRO resident, once his problems have been resolved or alleviated, contact with the Hotel Alert worker is usually broken. However, during his regular visit to the hotel, the worker can stop in and check on the senior and be available if a crisis should arise again.

The cost effectiveness of Hotel Alert is easy to measure. To provide an average of six hours of social work assistance to an older person costs our agency $70 (although not all individuals require that much casework time). If a senior is faced with a crisis that is not addressed, premature institutionalization is a real possibility. Costs of a board and care or nursing facility run in excess of $2000 a month, a tremendous burden on the taxpayer, not to mention loss of a person's dignity and independence. Without the Hotel Alert program, hundreds of seniors might have been faced with institutionalization, a tragic and personal loss to our community.

Although Hotel Alert was designed to address the problems in the San Diego SROs, it is a program that could easily be duplicated in cities throughout the United States. It taps into and utilizes the natural helping network that exists throughout our society. It stresses the importance of the volunteer, a precious and valuable resource. Most of all, it is a personalized and humanistic approach that emphasizes the importance of allowing the elderly to maintain an independent lifestyle.

Here is an example of the work we do. Mr. L. was found wandering the streets by the San Diego Police Department. He was brought to the Center in a squad car. Appearing very confused and weak, he had lunch at the congregate meal program. Afterwards, the Hotel Alert worker spoke with him at length. Because Mr. L. speaks broken English, the landlord was unable to understand him and had evicted him for non-payment of rent. It turns out that the hotel management company had recently changed and Mr. L. was unaware of it (he also had trouble reading English). He had continued sending his rent to the old management firm. The Hotel Alert worker found Mr. L. temporary shelter at a hotel (whose manager, Rocky, has a soft spot for seniors in distress). It was also discovered that Mr. L. had not been receiving his Social Security checks on a regular basis. Social Security was contacted and the proper forms filed. A visit to Mr. L.'s bank revealed $100 in his account. He had been unable to withdraw it due to his inability to communicate in English. Rocky will allow Mr. L. to stay at the hotel until his Social Security check arrives. Follow-up: Mr. L. is now relocated and has his own hotel room with a small refrigerator. He attends our Center occasionally for lunch and reports that he is quite happy.

Suggestions

1 Ask your local office of the Administration on Aging what programs are available to offer support to your elderly relative when you cannot be present.
2 Investigate the following resources:
   Health: American Medical Radio News (800)621-8094 offers prerecorded messages that highlight daily health news and feature stories. A service of the American Medical Association.
   National Health Information Clearinghouse: (800)336-4797, (703) 522-2590 in Virginia (call collect) provides a central source of information and referral for health questions. Staff members do not diagnose, recommend treatment, or make physician referrals. A service of the Office of Disease Prevention and Health Promotion, U.S. Department of Health and Human Services.

adapting to physical changes

In middle age, cells maintain a balance between making new cells and breaking down old cells. But as the body ages, breakdown is faster than replacement of cells, and so the signs and symptoms of aging become visible. There is progressive impairment of body function, which threatens independence.

Someone who has been a physical education teacher with pride in her active, well-coordinated body may develop a chronic neuromuscular disease. She loses control of body movement and becomes incontinent. She may need a walker, urinary catheters, and adult incontinence pads. Instead of active participation in sports, she will have to find alternative ways of expressing herself.

Family members need to show respect for a person's place in the family, especially when the elderly person is no longer achieving success in business and community affairs. Physical changes in the level of oxygenation in the blood cause tiredness, less enthusiasm, and less participation in social activities. Family encouragement will enable the older person to face the problems of a decrease in body function.

The family who knows the normal changes of aging will be more aware of what constitutes abnormal aging and seek help for it. In general, all body functions slow down and become less efficient. Conservation of energy is an important principle to follow. When I visited EPCOT Center in Orlando, Florida, I was pleased to see the number of families who were including a frail elderly relative in the family outing. Special services were available for elderly/disabled guests. Effort was being made to make the rides wheelchair accessible. Sight-impaired guests were issued complimentary cassettes and recorders.

Adaptation to Change

Adaptation is the result of the body fighting to regain the natural balanced state of the body. One force which upsets adaptation is change. Too many rapid changes exhaust adaptation energy. Scientists have found that people who have many rapid changes which they perceive to be important are more likely to become ill within a year. It appears that the folk wisdom that suggests a woman who is widowed should make no important changes for a year is correct.

Lack of Oxygen

In the elderly, the heart muscle becomes less efficient, reacting slowly to a need for an increase in cardiac output. It needs a longer period of rest between beats and does not contract as vigorously, due to a decrease in muscle strength. Blood vessels lose their elasticity, so it is harder for the heart to pump out blood against a higher pressure. The diameter of these vessels may also be clogged with fatty deposits on the walls. These changes lead to fatigue, due to a lack of sufficient oxygen and nutrients to the tissues.

The chest rib cage is more rigid, chest muscles become weaker and lungs are less elastic. A decrease in the cough reflex increases the potential for aspiration of foods into the lungs. Smoking and air pollution in combination with aging lead to a decrease in respiratory function. The walls of the lung air cells break down, resulting in fewer, larger air sacs with less wall surface area to absorb the oxygen. This leads to changes in the amounts of oxygen in the blood and tissues. However, if elderly people exercise and stop smoking, they can maintain better consumption of oxygen than younger people who smoke and do not exercise.

The brain needs a lot of oxygen. Without it, neuron cells die and are not replaced. Arteriosclerosis and clogged blood vessels can decrease blood flow to the brain. The aging brain takes longer to process information and to react to stimuli. There is a gap between neurons, and chemical neurotransmitters flow across these gaps, carrying messages. As the neurotransmitters decrease with aging, the brain function decreases. There is also a decrease in taste, smell, and in awareness of pain.

Body Temperature Problems

Fever is a sign of infection which warns a person that he is ill.

Because of inefficient control of function of body heat mechanisms, an older person may have an infection without having an elevated temperature or complaining of pain. The first sign of pneumonia may be that the person faints.

An environment which is too hot or too cold causes stress. The sweat glands of older people do not work as well, so they are more prone to heat stroke. Fever causes headache, dizziness, restlessness and confusion. A decreased sensation of thirst leads to dehydration.

An older person should dress appropriately and avoid very hot environments, to prevent heat stroke. It may be necessary to encourage the replacement of lost fluid and electrolytes, and give the person a cold sponging.

If an environment is too cold, a person produces heat by shivering. The superficial blood vessels constrict. In hypothermia the rectal temperature goes below 95°F. Hypothermia may be caused by exposure, impaired temperature regulating action, a decrease in body metabolism, inadequate heating, and/or immobility.

The person has a low temperature, is pale, not shivering, disoriented and restless, and the pulse and respiration are slow. To put the person in a hot bath would dilate the skin blood vessels, leading to a decrease in blood pressure, taking the blood away from vital areas. Gradually rewarm the person with blankets and give a warm drink. To prevent future problems, heat bedrooms and keep windows closed at night. If necessary, use an electric blanket.

Impaired Metabolism

Tooth decay affects ninety-eight percent of the U.S. population. Among persons sixty-five to seventy-four years of age with some natural teeth, two-thirds have gum disease. Snacks containing a high sugar content should be avoided, or else the person should thoroughly brush his teeth afterwards. Calculus is formed by the deposit of calcium from the saliva in neglected plaque on the teeth. Calculus requires scaling by the dentist.

Toothless people have no support for their face and look older. If people buy dentures, they often neglect dental appointments necessary to retain a good denture fit. Then the dentures become uncomfortable.

James Dubs, Deputy Director of the South Carolina Commission on Aging, informed me about the South Carolina Dental Association's dental discount program. People over sixty-five years, with an income less than sixty percent of the state's median family income and no dental insurance, receive a twenty percent discount on dental care. Check to see if your own state has a similar discount.

Food absorption in the small intestine is less efficient. There is less secretion of insulin from the pancreas, which can lead to a form of diabetes. The elderly person may need to be reminded to drink enough fluid. Constipation is a common problem, due to weakened intestinal muscles and insufficient fruit and fiber in the diet.

Bladder capacity decreases, which means that when a person feels that his bladder is full, he has less time to empty it before becoming incontinent. Men have problems with the enlarged prostate gland which can obstruct urination. Surgery may be necessary. The kidneys become less efficient in maintaining the body's natural chemical balance.

Immobility

The skin of a bedridden person can develop bedsores. The skin circulation is cut off due to pressure, particularly in areas where bones are close to the surface—elbow, hip, heels. Immobility causes a decrease in muscle strength and in muscle tissue. People decrease their activities because of fatigue. Posture becomes stooped.

Robert Heaney, M.D., of Creighton University communicated the following guidelines for prevention and treatment of osteoporosis, prepared by the American Society for Bone and Mineral Research. Osteoporosis is a bone disease characterized by a reduction in bone density accompanied by increasing brittleness, associated with loss of calcium from the bones. By age sixty-five, one quarter of all white women have had a fracture. Post-menopausal women are most susceptible.

Loss of bone mass develops gradually, due to lack of exercise, estrogen deficiency, poor nutrition, and especially calcium deficiency. Milk group foods are our most common source of calcium. Other sources of calcium include leafy green vegetables, sardines, almonds, shellfish and tofu. The Society for Bone and Mineral Research recommends that we follow these preventive measures:

(1) Get plenty of exercise.

(2) Eat calcium-rich foods.

(3) Avoid large amounts of vitamins unless prescribed.

(4) Avoid cigarette smoking.

(5) Take precautions to prevent falls—especially for the frail elderly.

(6) Discuss the potential use of estrogen replacement therapy with your physician.

Reduced Vision

The size of the pupil of the eye decreases with age, so the pupil does not let in as much light. The elderly need bright light to read. It takes time for the elderly to adapt from a brightly lit room to a less well-lit room. Color and depth perception decrease, which can lead to accidents.

The ability to focus on close objects or to see small print commonly declines after the age of forty. There is no known prevention, but the focusing problem can be compensated for with glasses. Another approach is through providing books in larger print.

G. K. Hall Publishing Company provides a Large-Print-Books-By-Mail program. This is a shop-at-home service, not a book club. Readers are under no obligation to buy when they receive the catalog. Hall offers best-selling fiction and nonfiction and favorite mystery, romance, and western authors—even cookbooks.

Flo Scholtes, coordinator, described how the Jackson-George Regional Library System is meeting the needs of clients with impaired vision:

> The mini-libraries were established three years ago. While displaying the large print books, a tall shabby but clean elderly woman wearing eye glasses approached me. I asked if she liked to read, but she said she couldn't see well enough anymore. I opened the large print book for her to see. Her face lit up. She joyfully exclaimed, "I can read it. Oh, can I take it home? I'll bring it right back." I explained that she could take as many as she liked and should return them to the site when read. She clasped the book to her and ran to lock it in her pick-up truck.
>
> We also have "Talking Books," for the blind and "Mail-A-Large Print Book" for the homebound. In each library there is a bulletin board with current information for senior citizens.

The elderly should have regular health check-ups to detect vision problems and systemic diseases, such as hypertension and diabetes, which may cause eye problems. A lack of balance between production of fluid and drainage of fluid in the eyeball causes excess fluid pressure in the eye (glaucoma). This pressure on the optic nerve gradually destroys vision. Eye drops to constrict the pupil help the fluid to drain; oral medications can reduce the fluid pressure; surgery, if needed, provides an outlet for drainage. Glaucoma does not usually show early symptoms, so routine eye exams are important. Later symptoms are a reduction in peripheral vision with slightly blurred vision.

Another common eye disease in the elderly is cataracts. These are opaque areas in the lens, which is normally transparent. Since light does not pass through the opaque areas, vision may become blurred, particularly peripheral vision. After the cataract surgery, a plastic lens is implanted in the eye. Should the eye fluid pressure be so high that there is a danger of the plastic lens coming out, the surgeon will not put in the plastic lens, but will prescribe special glasses or contact lenses after surgery. The National Society to Prevent Blindness, 79 Madison Avenue, New York, NY 10016 has free pamphlets. An example is *The Aging Eye: Facts on Eye Care for Older Persons.*

The American Optometric Association operates an Older Adult Eye Health Education and Screening Program. It is designed to educate older adults about how age affects vision, common vision problems, available treatment, and things to do to compensate for vision changes. The program also provides free vision screenings to identify those with signs of vision problems, or of general health problems—hypertension, diabetes etc.—that can affect their vision.

Vision and Driving Tips from the American Optometric Association

Approximately 32,200,000 persons age fifty-five and older drive, and according to the National Safety Council, when the number of miles driven is taken into account, they have a poorer accident record than drivers in their middle years. The most common violations of older drivers include failure to yield right-of-way and improper lane changes, passing, turning, and expressway driving. Since about ninety percent of driving decisions are based on what drivers see or think they see, changes in vision due to aging are often to blame. Older adults however, generally do not have to give up driving but they should recognize their limitations and adjust driving accordingly.

Generally, changes in vision may interfere with older drivers' abilities to see and recognize what is on the road ahead; to see effectively at night; to see against the glare of oncoming headlights and to recover quickly from glare; to judge distances between themselves and other vehicles or objects; and to detect movement from the side while looking straight ahead. To compensate for these changes, the American Optometric Association suggests older drivers do the following:

- Seek regular vision examinations to maintain proper vision for day and night driving.

- Avoid frames with wide side pieces that may block side vision.
- Wear quality sunglasses on sunny or bright, cloudy days.
- Never wear sunglasses, or fashion-tinted lenses, including yellow tinted lenses, when driving at night.
- Confine driving to places, speeds and hours in which they are comfortable and competent.
- Avoid driving at dusk.
- When driving at night, reduce speed; try to limit driving to well-lit or familiar roads; and keep headlights, taillights and turn signals clean and properly adjusted.
- Keep pace with the average traffic flow, going not too fast or too slow when driving.
- Avoid pulling off alongside the highway. If necessary, use the car's four-way emergency flashers.
- Choose a car with a clear rather than tinted windshield.
- Avoid drinking and driving. Alcohol can affect every vision skill needed for safe driving.
- Know the effects on vision of any prescription or non-prescription drugs being taken before getting behind the wheel.

The average sixty-year-old needs seven times as much light as the average twenty-year-old to perform the same tasks. The eyes' normal aging is behind this need for more light. It is also the reason why older eyes are usually more comfortable under incandescent rather than fluorescent bulbs. Older adults can compensate for this aging change by increasing light bulb wattage indoors; carrying a small flashlight when outdoors at night; and exercising care in low-lighted areas.

Some older adults may have difficulty seeing comfortably and clearly in more brightly lit areas. This can be a sign of a vision problem, such as a cataract developing in the center of the eye's lens, and a vision examination is in order.

Resources for the Blind

Marilyn Ali, Project Director, acquainted me with Services to Reach and Involve Visually Impaired Elderly (STRIVE), in the Virgin Islands:

(1) The objective of Project STRIVE is to establish extensive services geared towards reaching the blind, visually impaired, and/or handicapped elderly that reside in various sectors of our community at all levels of functioning.

    A. A homebound program for isolated and secluded elderly persons provides:

        1. Interview and evaluation

2. Friendly visiting
3. Referrals for yearly eye examination
4. Referrals for medical evaluation
5. Instruction in activities of daily living
6. Recreation activities with carry-over value in the home, i.e., arts and crafts, sewing, etc.
7. Braille instruction—when feasible
8. Mobility and orientation
9. Family involvement
10. Limited psychological services and limited social work services

B. A community service program provides services to persons with some limitations and those with more independent functioning. This program has provisions for group-recreational activities, i.e., crafts, cooking, exercise, trips, birthday parties, baking, weekly and daily religious services, shopping, and transportation.

(2) STRIVE emphasizes the need for implementation of services geared towards the prevention of blindness among the elderly. It provides training in effective methods of working with visually impaired and/or handicapped older persons, for staff and volunteers in age-related situations.

Ms. Ali perceives that "many times services to the blind reinforce dependency, they are too often geared to erroneous preconceived limitations in the mind of those who develop the services and do not allow for the participant to utilize existing capacities and to develop abilities and become more independent as they possibly can. Sometimes blind and handicapped persons tend to be segregated from the mainstream of the community by providing special programs for blind only, when they could fit into regular programs." Further information about local programs to aid visually impaired people is available from the local public health service.

Reduced Hearing

Sound energy moves through the air as a wave. Pitch is the frequency of the sound and loudness is the energy of the sound. The eardrum vibrates with the waves striking it and transmits these vibrations into the middle ear. Muscles contract when necessary to protect the nerve of the inner ear from very loud noises. Continued exposure to loud noise leads to hearing loss.

It has been estimated that approximately thirty percent of adults sixty-five through seventy-four, and about fifty percent of those age seventy-five through seventy-nine suffer some degree of hearing loss. More than ten million older people are hearing impaired. People with hearing impairments often withdraw socially to avoid the frustration and embarrassment of not being able to understand what is being said. In addition, hearing-impaired people may become suspicious of relatives and friends who "mumble" or "don't speak up." A ringing in the ears may be present. Social occasions are less fun, because the person cannot understand what is being said in a noisy environment.

In addition to loss of hearing cells and diminished hearing function due to aging, earwax or infection can block sound waves. Nerve damage can occur as a side effect of drugs or loud noises. Your doctor will determine the cause and recommend a specialist if necessary.

The National Institute on Aging's *Age Page* offers the following suggestions:

- Speak slightly louder than normal. However, shouting will not make the message any clearer, and may sometimes distort it. Speak at your normal rate, but not too rapidly.
- Speak to the person at a distance of 3 to 6 feet. Position yourself near good light so that your lip movements, facial expressions, and gestures may be seen clearly. Wait until you are visible to the hearing-impaired person before speaking. Avoid chewing, eating, or covering your mouth when speaking.
- Never speak directly into the person's ear. This prohibits the listener from making use of visual clues.
- If the listener does not understand what was said, rephrase the idea in short, simple sentences.
- Arrange living rooms or meeting rooms so that no one is more than 6 feet apart and all are completely visible.
- Treat the hearing-impaired person with respect. Include the person in all discussions about him or her. This helps to alleviate the feelings of isolation common in hearing-impaired persons.

A hearing aid amplifies sound to stimulate the nerve cells. Attitude and activation are important, since proper maintenance and regular check-ups are essential for the hearing aid to function. Lip-reading is a useful skill to acquire. Implants into the inner ear are being developed for deaf people, but although some sounds are heard, it is not yet possible to decode speech with these implants.

The National Institute of Neurological and Communicative Disorders and Stroke, Building 31, Room 8A06, Bethesda, Maryland 20205, is the focal point within the federal government for research on hearing loss and other communication disorders. Ask for the Institute's pamphlet *Hearing Loss: Hope Through Research*.

The Family and Physical Changes

The function of an elderly person deteriorates with time. Therefore it is not appropriate to apply the standards for normal function developed for assessing middle-aged persons to elderly people. Since the rate of change is gradual, the family may not even be aware of losses until they are far advanced. So it is necessary to be alert and look for the general signs of aging.

Of course, each individual has an individualized pattern of aging. In certain areas a person may show above average function when compared to his peers, whereas in other areas a person will show below average function. It is necessary to identify a person's areas of strength and build upon them, encouraging as much independence as possible. Once aware of the pattern of aging shown by your relative, assist him to cope with this pattern.

Visitors with colds or flu should be kept away from older people, since the elderly have less efficient immune systems and are very susceptible to infection. An acute illness will make the natural breakdown of cells worse. Aside from this, try to keep the relationships of your elderly relative as normal as possible. Acceptance of the fact that the elderly have more health problems and preparing for this potential situation in advance will reduce anxiety of the elderly and of their caregivers.

This does not mean that an elderly person should be waited on, if he is able to do things for himself. The doctor may prescribe adaptive equipment to enable the person to function independently. If possible the elderly person should participate in housework, like other members of the family. Throughout this book, there are examples of how different community associations assist elderly people to become involved in interesting activities, instead of staying home and worrying about their health problems.

Suggestions

1 Learn the physical changes in aging.
2 Investigate the following resources as needed:

<u>Vision Impairments</u>: American Council for the Blind (800) 424-8666, (202)393-3666 in DC, offers information on blindness. Provides referrals to clinics, rehabilitation organizations, research centers, and local chapters. Also publishes printed resource lists.

<u>Handicaps</u>: Library of Congress, National Library Services for the Blind and Physically Handicapped (800)424-8567, (202) 727-2142 in DC, guides individuals incapacitated by short- or long-term illness to libraries that utilize the talking book service and provides a listing of books and magazines in braille.

<u>Hearing and Speech</u>: Hearing Helpline (800)424-8576, (703) 642-0580, provides information on better hearing and the prevention of deafness. A service of the Better Hearing Institute.

<u>National Association for Hearing and Speech Action Line</u>: (800) 638-8255, (301)897-8682 in Hawaii, Arkansas, and Maryland, offers information on hearing and speech problems. Distributes materials on speech-language pathologists and audiologists certified by the American Speech-Language-Hearing Association, hearing aids and other topics related to hearing and speech.

preventing chronic illness

A person who participates in social activity and physical exercise is more likely to remain independent. Health check-ups every year may identify health problems at an early enough stage to be corrected and may indicate the need for immunizations against influenza and pneumonia or other preventive treatments. A nutritious diet can also build up a person's resistance to illness. An important role for the family is education—assisting your elderly relative to reduce chances of developing a chronic illness.

Causes of Chronic Illness

Health risks associated with the development of chronic illness in the elderly include:

- heredity factors associated with nervous system disease, heart disease and cancer
- environmental factors associated with polluted air and water, unsafe consumer products, driving hazards, noise, poor housing
- lifestyle factors associated with alcohol or drug misuse, lack of exercise, unsafe driving, poor eating, smoking, stress

Here are some suggestions from the Surgeon General to benefit your health:

(1) Eat sensibly. Avoid overeating and reduce the amount of fat, saturated fat, cholesterol, sugar and salt in your diet. When you snack, try fresh fruits and vegetables.

(2) Exercise regularly. Almost everyone can benefit from some form of exercise—and there's some form of exercise almost everyone can do. As little as thirty minutes of vigorous exercise three times a week will help to improve circulation and tone up sagging muscles. Proper rest is important too.

(3) Avoid addictions. Think twice about lighting that cigarette or taking that extra drink—particularly if you plan to drive. Take medications only when you have to—and if you are not sure, check with your doctor.

(4) Be safety conscious. Think "safety first" at home, at school, at work, at play, and on the highway. Buckle seat belts, keep poisons and weapons (especially handguns) out of reach of children, wear life jackets while boating, keep emergency numbers by the telephone.

(5) Learn to handle stress. Stress is an important part of living, and properly handled, it need not be a problem. However, unhealthy responses, such as driving erratically, chronic anger or fear, and drinking too much, are destructive and can cause a variety of physical and mental health problems. Learn to cope with stress: don't let worry and tension rob you of your capacity to enjoy life.

Occupational diseases may not be detected until people are old. They can be prevented by engineering controls or personal behavior controls. Engineering controls, e.g., housekeeping and sanitation, work twenty-four hours a day with minimal attention to guidelines for maintenance, whereas personal behavior controls are more difficult to implement. Worker education helps.

Levels of Prevention

Primary prevention attempts to remove the cause of a disease or to help the person become resistant to a disease. Prevention of illness is easier than the dramatic surgery or drug therapy when illness is established. For example, smoking and air pollution have been shown to be risk factors associated with respiratory disease. Therefore, it would be important to encourage people to stop smoking. To promote energy conservation, buildings were sealed. Now we recognize that this sealing can decrease the quality of the indoor air. We may have to accept energy loss, in order to prevent air pollution.

Cigarette smoking is responsible for approximately 320,000 deaths annually in the U.S. Smoking is the single most preventable cause of death and disease. It is associated with heart and blood vessel diseases, chronic bronchitis and emphysema, cancer, respiratory infections and stomach ulcers.

Smoking is a major contributor to death and injury from fires, burns and other accidents. Twenty-nine percent of fatal house fires and a substantial number of burn injuries are smoking related. Ten years after quitting cigarette smoking, the death rates for lung cancer and other smoking-related causes of death approach those of non-smokers. Here is an example of a successful antismoking program carried out in a private company.

Speedcall Corporation conducts a voluntary program based on the honor system. The company does not prohibit smoking except in areas containing flammable liquids and the like. One of the aspects of the program is that people are free to smoke during working hours; those who do not smoke at all during the 8–5 workday (including break and lunch times) will receive the $7.00 gross in the paycheck weekly. If someone "backslides" and smokes one week, the person is again eligible the following week to earn the bonus again for not smoking. The whole philosophy of the program is that it does not penalize smokers, only rewards those who do not smoke, and provides the necessary incentives, money award, and peer pressure.

Donald Shepard, Ph.D., of the Harvard School of Public Health conducted a survey of Speedcall's workers. He found that ninety-seven percent of employees thought that the program was a good idea. There was a fifty-nine percent decline in cigarette consumption. Speedcall's health claims per employee were about thirty percent below those expected— seventy-five percent for small employee groups as a whole.

Elderly persons are at risk for developing complications from influenza, if they have a chronic cardiac or pulmonary disease, since it weakens individuals and makes them vulnerable to pneumonia. To build up resistance to influenza, the Public Health Service recommends annual influenza injections for persons over sixty-five years.

Secondary prevention refers to the early diagnosis of disease and early prompt treatment. A health hazard appraisal screens people without illness symptoms for primary prevention, and also serves as an instrument for secondary prevention. Mary Weibling, a community health nurse from Independence, Missouri, sent me a copy of the results of an Older Adult Wellness Assessment, conducted from April through September, 1985, on 1000 Independence residents. (Further information about the Assessment is available from Ms. Weibling.) The percentages show what percentage of the respondents chose that particular option. The survey follows.

1. *Do you have back trouble?*   A) Yes 42%   B) No 58%
2. *Do you have arthritis?*   A) Yes 59%   B) No 41%
3. *Do you have diabetes?*   A) Yes   8%   B) No 92%
4. *Do you have high blood pressure?*   A) Yes 37%   B) No 63%
5. *Do you have a history of heart trouble?* A) Yes 26%   B) No 74%
6. *Do you have 3 or more colds a year?*   A) Yes 15%   B) No 85%
7. *When was the last time you had your blood pressure checked (before this screening)?*
   A) Past 6 months 86%   C) Twelve months or longer 5%
   B) 6–12 months 9%   D) Never 0%
8. *When was the last time you went to a physician specifically for a physical examination?*
   A) Within past year 63%   C) 3–5 years ago 9%
   B) 1–2 years ago 20%   D) 6 or more years ago 8%
9. *Have you had a tetanus/diphtheria booster shot within the past 10 years?*
   A) Yes 18%   C) Don't know 10%
   B) No 72%
10. *How much physical effort do you expend during the week?*
    A) Little (sitting or lying most of the time) 9%
    B) Moderate (walk to store, housework, walking in shopping mall) 78%
    C) Heavy (brisk walk/jog 1 mile or more, swimming year round) 13%
11. *How often do you participate in physical activities (walking, jogging, swimming)?*
    A) Seldom 37%   C) 3 or more days per week 39%
    B) 1–2 days per week 24%
12. *Do you have vision or hearing problems that have not been corrected?*
    A) No 64%   C) Yes, hearing only 12%
    B) Yes, vision only 16%   D) Yes, both vision and hearing 8%
13. *How often do you drink alcoholic beverages (number of times per week)?*
    A) Seldom or never 93%   D) 7 times per week 1%
    B) 1–2 times per week 4%   E) Only on weekends 0.5%
    C) 3–6 times per week 1.5%
14. *How many drinks do you usually have in one sitting?*
    A) I don't drink 90%   C) I have 2–4 drinks 4%
    B) I have a relaxing drink 5%   D) I have 5 or more drinks 1%

15. *Do you smoke?* A) Yes 20%   B) No 80%

16. *How often do you brush and floss your teeth?*
   A) Less than once a day 5%
   B) Once a day 33%
   C) Twice a day 27%
   D) After every meal 5%
   E) I have false teeth or no teeth 30%

17. *How many __total__ hours of sleep do you usually get in 24 hours (including catnaps)?*
   A) 6 hours or less 23%
   B) 7–8 hours 67%
   C) 9 or more hours 10%

18. *How often do you wear seat belts?*
   A) Seldom or never 46%
   B) Occasionally 26%
   C) Usually 28%

19. *Do you drive after or while drinking an alcoholic beverage?*
   A) Never 95%
   B) Occasionally 5%

20. *Do you look for and remove safety hazards in your home (throw rugs, loose carpet, electric cords, etc.)?*
   A) Yes 92%
   B) No 8%

21. *Do you restrict your eating of red meat, whole milk and butter?*
   A) Yes 63%
   B) No 37%

22. *Do you avoid salty foods (saltine crackers, bacon, ham, canned soup) and use salt sparingly?*
   A) Yes 64%
   B) No 36%

23. *How often do you eat a breakfast?*
   A) Rarely or never 7%
   B) Occasionally 10%
   C) Every day 83%

24. *How often do you eat sugary foods (cake, candy, cookies, soda pop, sugar coated cereal)?*
   A) Rarely or never 15%
   B) Occasionally 54%
   C) Every day 31%

25. *How often do you eat 2 servings from the __meat__ group (beef, fish, eggs, peanut butter, beans) in a day?*
   A) Rarely 14%
   B) Occasionally 39%
   C) Every day 45%
   D) Not sure 2%

26. *How often do you take __calcium__ tablets or eat 2 servings from the __milk__ group (cheese, cottage cheese, yogurt) in a day?*
   A) Rarely 8%
   B) Occasionally 25%
   C) Every day 66%
   D) Not sure 1%

27. *How often do you eat 4 servings of __fruit and vegetables__ in a day?*
   A) Rarely 8%
   B) Occasionally 28%
   C) Every day 61%
   D) Not sure 3%

28. *How often do you eat 4 servings from the __bread and cereal__ group (bread, noodles, rice, corn) in a day?*
   A) Rarely 12%
   B) Occasionally 26%
   C) Every day 60%
   D) Not sure 2%

29. *How often do you do things with others (visiting friends/relatives, church events, group activities, shopping, games)?*
   A) Seldom or never   3%   C) 1–2 times per week   33%
   B) Less than once per week   7%   D) 3 or more times per week   57%

30. *How often do you feel too tired to get out of bed or not want to do much of anything?*
   A) Rarely   54%   C) Usually   10%
   B) Occasionally   36%

31. *How often do you feel grief or sorrow over the loss of someone or something (spouse, child, pet, home, job)?*
   A) Rarely   38%   C) Usually   16%
   B) Occasionally   46%

32. *How often are you worried about things beyond your control?*
   A) Rarely   43%   C) Usually   13%
   B) Occasionally   44%

33. *Age:*
   A) 64 and under   20%   D) 80–89   20%
   B) 65–69   21%   E) Over 90   1%
   C) 70–79   38%

34. *Sex:*
   A) Male   29%   B) Female   71%

35. *Are you the guardian (responsible for) of any children under 18 years old?*
   A) Yes   6%   B) No   94%

36. *Have you had a rectal examination within the past year?*
   A) Yes   34%   B) No   66%

37. *Marital status:*
   A) Married   50%   C) Divorced   10%
   B) Single   7%   D) Widowed   33%

38. *Have you had a change in bowel or bladder habits?*
   A) No   78%   C) Yes, change in bladder
   B) Yes, change in bowel   habits   7%
      habits   9%   D) Yes, both   6%

39. *Height, in inches (Use the two lines on the computer card. Ask volunteer for help if you need it.):*

40. *Weight, in pounds (Use the three lines on the computer card.):*

41. *Do you experience any of the following: frequent urination during the night, excessive thirst, extreme hunger?*
   A) Yes   35%   B) No   65%

42. *Do you experience any of the following: pain or discomfort in your chest, arm, or jaw; unable to catch your breath, especially during physical activity?*
   A) Yes   26%   B) No   74%

43. *Do you experience any of the following: difficulty getting dressed or fixing meals, pain or discomfort in any of your joints?*
A) Yes   34%   B) No   66%

44. *Have you recently experienced any of the following: a sore that does not heal, unusual bleeding or discharge, obvious change in a wart or mole, nagging cough or hoarseness, indigestion or difficulty in swallowing?*
A) Yes   17%   B) No   83%

45. *How many different prescription medications are you presently taking?*
A) None   31%   D) Three   11%
B) One   27%   E) Four or more 12%
C) Two   19%

46. *How many non-prescription medicines or substances do you take a day (aspirin, vitamins, herbs, cold remedies)?*
A) None   35%   D) Three   8%
B) One   33%   E) Four or more 8%
C) Two   16%

For women only:

47. *How often do you check your breasts for lumps?*
A) Never   33%   C) Monthly   20%
B) Irregularly   45%   D) Not applicable (both breasts removed)   2%

48. *When was the last time you had a PAP smear taken?*
A) Within the past year   41%   D) 6 or more years ago   15%
B) 1–2 years ago   19%   E) Never   6%
C) 3–5 years ago   19%

Donald Goughler, Executive, Southwestern Pennsylvania Human Services Mobile Health Screening program, described the service: "We are a complete health screening program as we provide the following:

- detection of abnormalities
- documentation of abnormalities
- referral to your physician of choice

To help people to understand how the Health Screening is beneficial, they are given a pamphlet with information."

Each testing station has a paragraph about it in the pamphlet. Here are some examples:

Vision can be a problem at this stage of your life. You must be screened on a regular basis of every 2 or 3 years to determine and treat diseases of the eyes. For example, early detection of glaucoma can mean the difference between taking eye drops daily or becoming blind. Don't neglect your eyes.

Urinalysis is a good indication of body abnormalities, especially kidney and liver dysfunctions. We test through the use of specially treated dipsticks for seven different findings—sugar and/or blood in the urine are two of the most common abnormal findings.

The PAP test is an examination of cells that are being shed normally from two areas of a woman's uterus, the womb or body of the uterus, and the cervix or mouth of the womb. The loose cells collect in the vagina. They are gathered on a flat stick and cells are taken directly from the surface of the cervix. These cells are studied under a microscope. Uterine cancer sometimes gives no warning at all. That is why the PAP test is so extraordinarily valuable. It can find cancer when the chances of cure are the best.

The screening includes a history, height and weight, hearing, breast examination, oral screening, and blood testing. This latter includes twenty-five different blood tests. Together they form a pattern if a disease affecting the blood is present. Usually you must fast six hours, since food affects test results.

All abnormal findings are referred to the client's own doctor. If there are any abnormalities, the person is informed within one week. In addition, a medical social worker contacts the person within one month, to find out what the person and his doctor have decided to do about the screening results. All charts are kept on file.

The third level of prevention is tertiary prevention, which has the purpose of rehabilitating people with an established chronic disease to their highest level of wellness. It offers earlier, more effective management for persons experiencing discomfort, pain and distress. An example would be alcohol and drug rehabilitation programs. The elderly frequently take a broad variety of medications for multiple disease conditions. If any of these drugs interact with alcohol, they can cause harm to the person.

Accident Prevention

For the past ten years, more than 100,000 deaths per year have been reported in the accident category. Deaths are principally caused by motor vehicles, poisonings, falls, drownings, fires, and burns. Use of seatbelts, no smoking in bed and smoke alarms will help prevent accidents.

The elderly are at risk for accidents because of poor vision and hearing. They may also have decreased muscular coordination and slower reflexes. Elderly cooks are more likely to burn themselves because of moving more slowly in reaction to a painful stimulus. Also, the decreased sensation of touch and pain means that it takes longer for pain to be recognized as a warning. Their sense of balance may be diminished, leading to falls and fractures. An assistive device, such as a cane or walker, may be needed.

Joseph Granados, Chief of Operations, provided information about Life Safety Systems. This System was researched and developed as a result of a joint commitment on the part of the International Association of Fire Fighters and the Muscular Dystrophy Association to provide a solution to an increasing life safety problem for the elderly and handicapped. Granados stated:

> The System is a newly developed automatic residential alarm network. It connects the homes of the aged and disabled with a computerized receiver at the fire department to provide instant contact in emergencies. Use of the System enables the municipality to deliver an improved level of service to a target population with a legitimate need. This is accomplished at low cost without additional personnel, thereby increasing productivity.
>
> The elderly (over sixty-five) and the disabled suffer a disproportionate rate of fire related deaths and injuries. This is due in part to the following:
>
> - An ever increasing number of disabled and elderly persons are residing in private homes because of a national emphasis on de-institutionalization.
> - There are dangerous delays in exiting to safety associated with the kind of physical impairment that comes with advanced age or disability.
> - Behavioral responses often decline with age and disability, increasing the chance of confusion and disorientation in emergency situations.
>
> In addition to greater risk from fire related traumas, it is also true that advanced age and disability increase the likelihood of unreported medical emergencies. These factors make a strong case for legitimate concern for the survival of the elderly and disabled in emergency situations.

Gordon Walker, Executive Director, and Joyce Deily, Occupational Therapy Coordinator, described the Jefferson Area Board for Aging Home Safety Program:

> We feel that the Home Safety Program fosters independence by helping to prevent the disproportionate share of home accidents suffered by

adults sixty-five and over. Although they make up only eleven percent of the population, they account for twenty-eight percent of home fire fatalities and eighty-two percent of fatal falls in the home.

There are many ways to prevent home accidents, either through the use of such safety equipment as a bathtub grab bar, or by teaching older adults task adaptations to compensate for age-related changes, but unfortunately many people are not aware of these preventive methods, or may not be able to afford their cost. For a typical Jefferson Area Board for Aging client who lives on just over $300/month, the price of a $35 bathtub rail is prohibitive. By providing such equipment for our clients on a long-term basis, we feel we are helping to reduce their risk of disabling injury and possible hospitalization and/or long-term care. We would like to see the Home Safety Program instituted on a widespread basis.

The Home Safety Program consists of two components:

(1) safety improvement for individual homes
(2) community education

Safety Improvements

The coordinator, an occupational therapist, visits the home to determine what safety hazards exist. Danger areas under consideration include falls, burns, and misuse of medication. Needed corrections are made by the therapist, the program handyman, or volunteers, e.g., marking a stove dial so it can be clearly seen by someone with failing eyesight, or the installation of a stairway hand rail or bathroom grab bar. Loose scatter rugs are affixed securely to the floor. Bathroom safety equipment such as a raised toilet seat or bathtub bench is given to low-income clients on a long-term loan basis, and names of appropriate clients are given to a local civic group that agreed to install free smoke detectors for low-income elderly homeowners. Volunteer and community involvement in correcting home hazards has been encouraged. Workers from the local electric power company have helped in replacing broken lamp and appliance switches, electric cords, etc., and students from a vocational-technical school made forty wooden chair-leg extenders to help physically debilitated elderly clients. Three church groups took up a collection to pay for the cost of materials for broken sidewalk replacement for two clients (previously unknown to them) and also supplied manpower for the job. During the first three months of the Home Safety Program's existence, until a paid handyman was hired, three volunteer carpenters made all necessary safety repairs and still act as back-up and consultants. An area medical supply company donated several pieces of equipment, and two local building firms have given lumber for various projects.

Discharge planning staff and therapy departments in area hospitals and nursing homes have been contacted for referrals of home-going patients who were hospitalized because they had fallen and are therefore considered particularly at risk. Presentations about the program were also made to Health Department nurses, and to Home Care workers, Aging Services Specialists, and nursing students. From July 1, 1984, to June 30, 1985, the first year of the Home Safety Program's operation, 114 clients received home assessments.

Community Education

A slide show on Home Safety for Older Adults, demonstrating various house and task safety modification for age-related changes, has been developed. Many of the suggested adaptations can be accomplished at very little cost, e.g., painting the bottom basement step a light or bright color so it can be more easily seen (since most stairway falls occur there in dim light), or storing internal and external medicines on separate shelves of the medicine chest and keeping a magnifying glass nearby if reading small print is a problem. A do-it-yourself Home Safety Checklist and a small booklet of safety tips for clients with limited reading skills have also been produced as handouts for educational presentations.

Care Assurance System for the Aging and Homebound (CASA) is a volunteer ministry in Alabama. Each county CASA is funded by local religious, civic, social groups and individuals. It seeks to fill gaps in the local social service delivery system. CASA reported the following case study:

> A ninety-one-year-old, blind black man called to say that his kitchen floor "felt strange" when he walked near his stove and hot water heater. A CASA volunteer home repair team went to his home and found that the supports underneath the house were rotten and the floor had completely separated from the back wall of his house. The floor was slanted in such a way that the hot water heater had nearly fallen through the hole into his backyard. They also found that a prowler had entered his home by breaking out his bedroom window after nearly tearing his back door from the hinges.
>
> The team put in a whole new window facing and window, repaired his door and replaced his floor and the supports under his house. They also found that his hot water heater was a fire hazard and it was repaired. The

man was so pleased with the work done and with volunteers who did it that he wanted to volunteer for CASA telephone reassurance. He now talks to another elderly blind man each day and they have become good friends. The team is now working on replacing his front porch which had rotted because of unrepaired leaks.

Suggestions

1 Identify potential safety hazards in your home and eliminate them.
2 Investigate the following resources:
   Motor Vehicle Passenger Safety: National Highway Traffic Safety Administration (800)424-9393, (202)426-0123 in DC, provides information and referral on the effectiveness of occupant protection, such as the use of safety belts and auto safety recalls. Staffed by technical experts who investigate consumer complaints and provide assistance in resolving problems. Gives referrals for consumer questions on warranties, service, sales, and auto safety regulations.
   Product Safety: Consumer Product Safety Commission (800) 638-CPSC, (800)638-8270, (800)492-8104, answers questions and provides free material on different aspects of consumer product safety, including product hazards, product defects, and injuries sustained as a result of using products.

exercise

Elderly people who have limitations of mobility are at risk for multiple health problems. Their muscles atrophy, joints become stiff, and calcium leaves their bones, leading to osteoporosis and fractures. When a person is walking around, the calf muscles act as a second heart, stimulating the blood vessels to keep the circulation going. Without this stimulation, blood will pool in the legs, and form dangerous clots. These clots can become dislodged and block off circulation to parts of the heart, lungs, and brain, depending upon where they lodge and on how much circulation they stop.

Pooling of respiratory secretions can lead to infection. Pooling of urine in the kidney and bladder can lead to infection and stones. The rhythmic movement of the gastrointestinal tract is disrupted, slowing stomach emptying and causing constipation.

Americans get little exercise. Housework or bowling do not produce the benefits of regular vigorous exercise, such as swimming, brisk walking, or running. These are aerobic activities—the body uses oxygen to produce the energy needed for the activity.

Benefits of Exercise

Exercise will help you to feel better and look better because it:
- gives you more energy
- helps in coping with stress
- helps prevent anxiety and depression
- helps prevent insomnia
- tones your muscles
- helps you stay at your desired weight

To lose one pound, you need to burn off 3500 calories more than you take in—eat less calories and exercise more.

Even people confined to bed can benefit from exercises to maintain body function and prevent the loss of function through disuse. Conscientious exercising means that when the person is able to resume walking again, he will not be held back in his rehabilitation because of stiff, immovable joints. Active motion is movement by the patient. Passive motion is movement of a part of the body by the caregiver. The physical therapist will show the family member how to assist his elderly relative to do the exercises prescribed by the doctor.

Range of motion exercises move the joint through its full movement. These exercises can be either active or passive motion. The full range is different for each joint, depending upon the type of joint and its normal function. For example, a hinge joint—the knee—consists of two bones which allow bending and straightening in one direction, whereas a ball-and-socket joint—the hip—allows movement in all directions.

If the range of motion (ROM) is not maintained, joints become stiff. Contractures develop with a permanent contraction of the muscle and fibrosis of the tissue surrounding the joint. Once these contractures have developed, then surgery is necessary to cut through the fibrosis, perhaps followed by a tendon transplant. Caregivers should not carry out ROM past the point where pain is experienced, or attempt to force the ROM past a contracture. Since elderly people suffer from osteoporosis, the caregiver would be more likely to break the bone before breaking through the contracture. The number of repetitions of the joint movements will be ordered by the doctor, to maintain muscle strength and endurance. Exercising improves blood circulation, to offset swelling of the ankles. The change of position helps prevent bedsores.

A healthy heart becomes stronger with exercise. Aerobic exercise elevating the pulse rate for thirty minutes of continuous activity three times a week trains the heart. Consult a physician before starting any exercise program, to find out what exercise program to aim for, given your age, sex, and condition. The doctor will also tell you what is an appropriate increase in the pulse rate with exercise.

There are general guidelines for older people using a target zone of sixty to seventy-five percent of a person's maximum heart rate:

Age	Target Zone	Average Maximum Heart Rate
65	93–116 beats per min.	155
70	90–113 beats per min.	150

The maximum heart rate is usually calculated as 220 minus your age. However, the elderly are a group in which members show great diversity. While ninety-three beats per minute might be safe for some healthy sixty-five-year-olds, others would be wise to aim for a slower rate, because of their health status. That is why the doctor needs to individualize the exercise program.

The following table is from *Exercise and Your Heart*, a publication you can order from the National Heart, Lung and Blood Institute. A person burns up only a minimal amount of calories with daily activities such as sitting. Any physical activity in addition to what you normally do will burn up extra calories. Below are the average calories spent per hour by a 150-pound person. (A lighter person burns fewer calories; a heavier person burns more.) Since precise calorie figures are not available for most activities, the figures below are averaged from several sources and show the relative vigor of the activities.

Bicycling 6 mph	240 cals
Bicycling 12 mph	410 cals
Cross-country skiing per hour	700 cals
Jogging 5½ mph	660 cals
Jogging 7 mph	920 cals
Jumping rope per hour	750 cals
Running in place per hour	650 cals
Running 10 mph	1280 cals
Swimming 25 yards/minute for an hour	275 cals
Swimming 50 yards/minute for an hour	500 cals
Tennis-singles per hour	400 cals
Walking 2 mph	240 cals
Walking 3 mph	320 cals
Walking 4½ mph	440 cals

Exercising harder or faster for a given activity will only slightly increase the calories spent. A better way to burn up calories is exercising longer and/or covering more distance.

Exercise Programs

Penny Carver, Program Director, told me about "Keep Moving," which was designed by the Executive Office of Elder Affairs in Massachusetts, to promote fitness, exercise, and socialization for adults fifty years and older. As part of the "Keep Moving" program, a state-wide network of Walking Clubs has been initiated. Persons interested in starting a Walking Club in their community are trained and certified as leaders. Club members receive "Keep Moving" membership certificates, passbooks to log their times and distances walked, and walking manuals. Leaders also receive certificates, posters to promote their club and T-shirts for enrolling ten club members. Carver stated:

> Three thousand older adults were joined by participants from New Hampshire, Rhode Island, Virginia and San Francisco at last year's Governor's Cup one-mile fun walk and three-mile competitive walk. A regular program of brisk walking prevents and manages several major health concerns of older people—coronary heart disease, hypertension, obesity, diabetes, anxiety, depression, arthritis, and osteoporosis.
>
> A regular walking program can slow down the aging process and add years of vigorous living. It energizes and increases stamina and strength. It helps control weight. For example, 100 extra calories a day can result in a ten pound weight gain. These extra calories can be burned by a fifteen to twenty minute walk each day. It tones muscles that would otherwise become flabby, helps maintain a sense of balance and agility, lessening the likelihood of injuries from falls or accidents, and improves self-image and a sense of self-reliance. It is advisable to inform your physician of your intentions and follow his or her advice.
>
> Brisk walking is an aerobic exercise. If you accelerate while walking, breathing automatically becomes faster and deeper, thus strengthening the heart and lungs and improving endurance—like more traditional aerobic exercises.
>
> Essential to safe brisk walks is the warm-up or activity just prior to a workout. People can achieve the warm-up by slow walking for five or ten minutes. Gradually stepping up the pace elevates your body temperature, pulse rate, and respiratory rate, and begins to stretch muscles, tendons and ligaments, thus reducing the chance of injury. This kind of warm-up can be followed by slow, smooth stretching exercises.
>
> As for post-workout activity, you should give your body the same time to react to its changing environment as you did when you did your warm-up. The post-workout or "cool down" time helps your body's transition to a resting state and should take between five and ten minutes. Gradually decrease the speed of your walk in order to give your heart, body temperature and muscles a chance to return to their normal state.
>
> If you are in good shape, the time you can walk and the pace will be different than someone who has been relatively inactive. For the greatest benefits, in the best circumstances, you should walk for at least thirty minutes, three times every week. Start each walk at a gradual pace for five minutes, increasing your speed when you feel comfortable to do so. But above all, be patient—it may take many weeks before brisk walking for a duration of fifteen to twenty minutes can be achieved.

How does the body normally respond to a new exercise program? An exhilarating feeling, deeper and quicker breathing and an accelerated heart beat are indications you are on the right track. Mild to moderate sweating, muscle aches and soreness are also normal responses to a new exercise program. A good warning signal is the "talk test." If you are unable to comfortably carry on a conversation while walking, slow down the pace considerably.

Extreme shortness of breath, very painful muscles, excessive perspiration, blueness of fingers or lips, irregular or fluttering heart beats, failure of a pulse to slow down, chest discomfort, light-headedness, dizziness, lack of coordination and nausea are all signals that tell you to stop exercising. A health care specialist should be consulted for any of these symptoms.

A slower heart rate, in a resting state, is a signal of an improved cardiovascular system. You should avoid aerobic walking on a full stomach, allowing two to three hours after a full meal, avoid exercise during illness or injury, and avoid physical exertion during high humidity, extreme heat or cold.

The following is adapted from *Exercise and Your Heart*, U.S. Department of Health and Human Services, 1981.

A Walking Program

Week #	Warm Up Walk Slowly	Target Zone Exercising Walk Briskly	Cool Down Walk Slowly	Total Time
1	5 min.	5 min.	5 min.	15 min.
2	5 min.	7 min.	5 min.	17 min.
3	5 min.	9 min.	5 min.	19 min.
4	5 min.	11 min.	5 min.	21 min.
5	5 min.	13 min.	5 min.	23 min.
6	5 min.	15 min.	5 min.	25 min.
7	5 min.	18 min.	5 min.	28 min.
8	5 min.	20 min.	5 min.	30 min.
9	5 min.	23 min.	5 min.	33 min.
10	5 min.	26 min.	5 min.	36 min.
11	5 min.	28 min.	5 min.	38 min.
12	5 min.	30 min.	5 min.	40 min.

If you want to become involved in a different exercise program, in addition to your walking program, here are a couple of suggestions. The American Alliance for Health, Physical Education, Recreation, and Dance is located at 1900 Association Drive, Reston, Virginia

22091. The Alliance will send you the booklet, *Fifty Positive Vigor Exercises for Senior Citizens*. Little equipment is needed—frisbee, bicycle inner tube or similar inexpensive items. The exercises are pleasant and enjoyable physical activities, even for the less active elderly.

Another exercise program is *The Fitness Challenge in the Later Years*, a product of the President's Council on Physical Fitness and Sports. This booklet offers three different exercise programs. "Red" is the easiest, "White" more difficult, and the "Blue" program is the most difficult and sustained. You can order *Fitness* from the Superintendent of Documents, U.S. Government Printing Office, Washington, DC 20402.

Helen Boosalis, Director, furnished information about Nebraska's Heritage Planters. In her words the purpose of the group is to:

> provide a way for older Nebraskans to remain active in their communities through tree planting. In addition, there are several related purposes which include:
>
> - increasing awareness as to the need to plant trees
> - increasing awareness of the role that older persons have played in the past and can continue to play if provided opportunities and options
> - the opportunity for older people to interact with younger generations through the tree planting projects
>
> This helps the elderly to conduct a project which can give them some visibility in their communities and to help dispel the myths that older persons are an obsolete resource. The older citizens improve the environmental quality and continue a legacy of service. The older groups have a chance to continue to exercise their energy, creativity, and experience with innovative projects, and often those projects are carried out with involvement of other segments of the community (youth groups, civic clubs, etc.).
>
> One group included residents of a nursing home. Another group beautified the rear yard of their senior center and turned it into a patio. Another group built an arboretum around a nursing home for the enjoyment of residents and community alike. The limited funds available in small grants has generated several times the value through additional local contributions of volunteer labor, cash contributions and plant material at reduced or no-cost rates. By agreeing to provide continuing maintenance to their projects, the seniors exhibit for others the lasting value of making commitment to their communities and to those who will follow in the years to come.

Lloyd Wright is President of the National Senior Sports Association (NSSA). According to him, the NSSA is a nonprofit organization dedicated to helping fifty-plus Americans maintain and improve their physical and emotional health through active sports participation. NSSA's main programming activity is the conduct of recreational and competitive events in golf, tennis, bowling and other sports at popular resorts around the world. Wright described the NSSA thusly:

> My original impulse was to encourage the active life among seniors, and to use group purchasing power to enable them to fulfill their retirement dreams of travel and sports. (In the 1970s, those dreams were being shattered by rampant inflation.)
>
> We now have 8,000 members. Loss and loneliness are the most constant companions of age. NSSA ministers to that reality by encouraging members to become active, creating opportunities for group gettogethers, expanding friendships. While I thought initially of the physical health benefit, I'm now convinced that the emotional benefits are more important. NSSA is not a singles organization, but many single men and women do belong.

In addition, there are disabled members, who enjoy participating in their desired sport.

Suggestions

1 Encourage your relative to participate in daily exercise.
2 Investigate the following resource:
  Sports: Women's Sports Foundation (800)227-3988, (415)563-6266 in Arkansas, Hawaii, and California, provides information on women's sports, physical fitness, and sports medicine.

nutrition and aging

Elderly people have less food intake, but with decreased activity, obesity can be a problem. Since there is a decrease in the senses of smell and taste, the elderly need highly seasoned food. Isolation and poverty can lead to inadequate nutrition. Persons in a nursing home may find that the home does not allow them to have a diet which allows for their cultural eating habits.

Deficits of essential nutrients can lead to several specific diseases or disabilities and increased susceptibility to others. Consumption of some nutrients may lead to conditions such as obesity, heart disease, diabetes of adult onset, hypertension, dental decay, and possibly some types of cancer. A well-balanced diet for a healthy person with no diet restrictions should include:

- two servings of milk or dairy products, such as cheese, cottage cheese, or yogurt
- two servings of protein-rich foods, such as lean meat, poultry, fish, eggs, beans, nuts, or peanut butter
- four servings of fruits and vegetables, including a citrus fruit or juice and a dark green leafy vegetable
- four servings of breads and cereal products (made with whole-grain or enriched flours), rice, or pasta

Large doses of some nutrients can act like drugs, often with serious results. Large amounts of vitamins A and D are particularly dangerous. Too much vitamin A can cause headaches, nausea and liver and bone damage. High doses of vitamin D can cause kidney damage in adults. Excessive amounts of iron can reach harmful levels in the kidney.

Adequate Nutrition

Protein is required by the body for building and maintaining body tissues. Meat, fish, poultry, milk, cheese, and eggs are all sources of high quality protein. Vegetable proteins can be combined to improve the quality of protein in a meal. Legumes (peas and beans) contain better quality than other vegetable sources.

Amino acids are the building blocks of protein. There are nine essential amino acids that must be provided in food, because the body cannot make them. Milk contains all nine essential amino acids. One of these acids, tryptophan, is being investigated as an aid to sleep, but it has not yet been approved as a medicine for this purpose.

Carbohydrates are made of carbon, hydrogen and oxygen. The complex carbohydrates, e.g., starch, are made up of simple sugars. Carbohydrates provide energy for the body. Cereal grains, legumes, and potatoes are good sources of starch.

Fats made up of fatty acids and glycerol are a source of energy and are essential for proper growth. They carry fat soluble vitamins. Unsaturated fatty acids are liquid oils at room temperature. Linoleic acid is an essential fatty acid, which must be obtained from food.

Vitamins are necessary in small amounts for normal growth and maintenance. Synthetic vitamins are identical to natural vitamins. A reasonable diet should provide sufficient vitamins without supplementary vitamins. Taking excess vitamins can be harmful.

Fat-soluble vitamins are stored in the liver. Vitamin A is necessary for new cell growth and vision. Vitamin D aids in the absorption of calcium and phosphorus. Vitamin E prevents oxygen from destroying other substances. It acts as a preservative. Vitamin K is essential for blood clotting.

Water-soluble vitamins are retained for short periods only. Vitamin C is the least stable vitamin. It promotes growth and tissue repair. The B complex vitamins and pantothenic acid are required for normal growth, maintenance, and energy. Folic acid and Vitamin B^{12} are necessary for the manufacture of red blood cells. Strict vegetarians need to supplement their diet with Vitamin B^{12}, since it is not present in sufficient amounts in plants.

Minerals have building and regulating functions. Some minerals are needed in large amounts—calcium, phosphorus, sodium, chloride, potassium, magnesium, and sulfur. Calcium is concentrated in the bones and teeth. It is important for nerves, nervous function and blood clotting. Phosphorus is also concentrated in the bones and teeth.

Sodium and potassium help maintain water and electrolyte balance. Sodium is present in most processed food. Excessive sodium intake can lead to water retention. Chloride is part of hydrochloric acid and aids in digestion. Magnesium is an essential part of enzyme systems. Sulfur is related to protein nutrition.

Trace minerals are needed in small amounts. For example, iron is necessary for transporting oxygen to body cells. Few foods contain iron in the necessary amounts. Liver is a good source.

U.S. Dietary Goals

The Select Committee on Nutrition and Human Needs includes the following goals:

(1) To avoid overweight, consume only as many calories as are expended; if overweight, decrease energy intake and increase energy expenditure.

(2) Increase the consumption of complex carbohydrates and naturally occurring sugars to about 48 percent of energy intake.

(3) Reduce the consumption of refined and processed sugars to about 10 percent of the total energy intake.

(4) Reduce overall fat consumption to about 30 percent of energy intake.

(5) Reduce saturated fat consumption to account for about 10 percent of total energy intake.

(6) Reduce cholesterol consumption to about 300 mg. a day.

(7) Limit the intake of sodium by reducing the intake of salt to about 5 grams a day.

The goals suggest the following changes in food selection and preparation:

(1) Increase consumption of fruits and vegetables and whole grains.

(2) Decrease consumption of refined and other processed sugars and foods high in such sugars.

(3) Decrease consumption of foods high in total fat, and partially replace with polyunsaturated fats.

(4) Decrease consumption of animal fat, and choose meats, poultry, and fish which will reduce saturated fat intake.

(5) Substitute low-fat and non-fat milk for whole milk, and low-fat dairy products for high-fat dairy products.

(6) Decrease consumption of butterfat, eggs, and other high cholesterol sources. Some consideration should be given to easing the cholesterol goal for the elderly in order to obtain the nutritional benefits of eggs in the diet.

(7) Decrease consumption of salt and foods high in salt content.

Persons with physical and/or mental ailments who have reason to believe that they should not follow guidelines for the general population should consult with a medical nutrition expert.

Food Budget

A shift to the dietary goals outlined offers potential for significant reduction in food costs. Savings may be achieved through home preparation and through reduction of and substitution for fats, refined and processed sugars, and expensive, fatty protein sources. Selected legumes and grain products provide the daily protein allowance for less than one dollar, whereas the majority of meat protein sources cost over one dollar a day.

Within the category of grain products, choosing the less processed, more nutritious products may often mean a savings. For instance, in one sampling, brand name converted rice cost twenty-five percent more than the low-priced store brand of instant rice. Slightly processed hot cereals like oatmeal are generally less expensive than ready-to-eat cereals. The most dramatic savings made by a reduction in sugar consumption result from cutting back on or eliminating purchases of candy, sweet baked goods, and soft drinks. Costs are also cut when the consumer chooses the unsweetened as opposed to the presweetened version of a particular food item; the prime example is breakfast cereals.

Reducing fat consumption, and particularly consumption of saturated fats, may also yield cost savings in several areas. For example, chicken or turkey, which are lower in saturated fat than meats, may average less than half the price of the beef, pork, and lamb cuts. Butter, on a per teaspoon basis, is generally more expensive than even the most costly of the unsaturated vegetable oils. Reduced use of prepared salad dressing, catsup, and sauces can not only cut expenses but reduce fat and/or salt and sugar consumption.

Greater home preparation can also yield savings in some areas as well as greater control over diet composition. A recent study by the Department of Agriculture comparing the costs of various convenience foods with their home-prepared counterparts found that out of twenty-five meat dishes tested, twenty-one were more expensive per serving when purchased ready-made. Many of the cost differentials were dramatic. The report said:

> The cost of home-prepared batter-dipped chicken was less than one-third that of the convenience products. Both chicken a-la-king frozen in a pouch and canned chicken salad spread, were about sixty percent more expensive per serving. . . . Consumers paid approximately forty cents more per serving for frozen turkey dinner or tetrazine than for the separate ingredients.

Many will find it impossible to change food preparation patterns drastically. However, it is evident that home preparation can offer savings as well as nutrition advantages.

Meals on Wheels

Ivan Simonsen, of the Western Idaho Regional County Council on Aging, wrote to me about their meals on wheels program:

> I am the Nutrition Director of eight counties—18 Senior Citizen Centers spread throughout rural southwestern Idaho. We serve the congregate meals and the Meals on Wheels to the elderly homebound. We needed to look for a facility where we could get good nutritional food at a reasonable price. The Weiser hospital is having a struggle to keep their doors open. They welcomed our plan for them to prepare the meals on our off days.
>
> Elderly folk want to stay in their own surroundings just as long as possible. They are extremely independent and their desire is to stay that way. However, the daily intake of sufficient and adequate food can become a real problem. The following can present major setbacks:
>
> (1) Shopping for groceries—often the elderly have to depend on someone else to do this.
> (2) Preparation of food—opening cans, packages, reading labels, reading dials on stove, over- and under-cooking, burning food, smelling and tasting food, food storage, leftovers and disposal of garbage.
> (3) The desire to cook in the first place.
> (4) After cooking—the real desire to eat.
> (5) Results are the habit of least resistance, leading to poor nutrition.
>
> Meals brought to the home provide:
>
> - nutritional foods (special diet when necessary)
> - daily scheduling

- a "person" contact at least once each day
- low cost
- written nutrition education
- special announcements of community happenings and other elderly programs that are available

The recipients say: "It's the bright spot in the day; I watch and wait for the meal to come; I have a new friend; I can stay in my own home; it's convenient."

Here are the advisory board nutrition committee's suggested criteria for recipients of home delivered meals:

- persons who are homebound because of a chronic physical or mental illness and have no one to cook for them
- persons who are homebound because they are unable to drive and unable to get into a car or van to attend congregate meals
- persons who are at an advanced age and are at a nutritional risk because they are unable to cook
- persons who are at an advanced age who have lost the desire or interest in preparing proper meals
- persons who are unable to get to the store to shop and unable to shop
- persons suffering from a nutritional deficiency because of not being able to cook the correct foods
- persons needing a special diet that they are unable to cook themselves
- persons who are unable to use their appliances in a safe manner
- persons who are just released from a hospital or a nursing home and referred by a physician
- persons who are handicapped
- persons whose economic and/or living conditions are such that they warrant home delivered meals, i.e., living in one room without appliances

Kathy Chandler-Henry, Director of Senior Programs, stated the following about Colorado Mountain College's nutrition program, Chat'n' Chew:

Meals are served every Tuesday and Friday at noon at a senior center. Noon meals are served each Tuesday and Thursday at a different center. Experienced cooks prepare meals at both sites, and all meals meet federal nutritional requirements. Menus are published in advance in the local newspapers and announced on radio stations.

There is no charge for the meals, but seniors who are able are requested to make a $1.25 donation. Guests under sixty are welcome, the charge for guest meals is $3. In addition, seniors work as volunteers at the meal sites, gather early to play cards, socialize and meet friends over lunch, and stay after the meals for project groups, bingo games, films or dances. Transportation is available to either meal site on the Traveler vans from anywhere in Garfield county.

On Dial-a-Ride days, seniors can call their Senior Center office and request a ride. They use the vans to go to doctor appointments, grocery shopping, and visiting friends. This van is their only source of transportation. There is no charge for this service, but seniors pay what they can afford.

James Drake furnished data on the Tri-County Senior Nutrition Project:

> Sometimes elderly clients who need home delivered meals also need help in other areas. The following is an example of a client who experienced a broad spectrum of continuing care services, eventually requiring nursing home care. However, independence was the primary goal until there were no other options.
>
> Margaret (fictitious name) actually became a client in 1978. She had Lou Gehrig's disease and knew that one day she would need institutional care. However, she wanted to remain completely independent for as long as possible and never become a worry or burden to her children who lived in other parts of the country. She was a retired nurse and did volunteer work for the Health Assessment program. As her disease progressed over the years, she began to experience muscular loss and advanced from a cane, to a walker, to a wheelchair. The Community Service Advisor assisted her in obtaining housing in an elderly/handicapped housing authority complex. The Elder Watch program was then contacted to complete a care plan for Margaret. For a while Margaret could cook some meals. Neighbors agreed to help her daily with dressing, turning down her bed, grocery shopping assistance, and light housekeeping chores. She gradually became more and more bedridden. Her income from Social Security and a pension from Civil Service placed her slightly over the income criteria for state assistance in a nursing home. Lou Gehrig's disease is not a recognized Medicare covered disease; therefore, she was ineligible for desperately needed home health services.
>
> A home-delivered meal was provided and a neighbor assisted in the feeding. Chore services were provided by the Elder Watch STEP employees. Elder Watch contacted Muscular Dystrophy Association in Dallas and obtained some medical equipment assistance and training. Since she received only about $560 per month, she could not afford nursing home care. The Community Service Advisor tried to get assistance from Senator Bentsen to see if the Civil Service pension could be waived in order to lower her income. However, he was unable

to help. Every possible resource in the community was tapped. However, she knew she needed institutional care as she could no longer move and she became incontinent.

Through careful and persistent negotiation, Elder Watch and the Advisor were able to identify a regional nursing home that would accept her at $550 per month rate. This is a greatly reduced rate for nursing home care. Margaret was pleased as she was able to participate in the negotiation and to view the nursing homes first hand. She was able to be a part of the selection and negotiation process.

Obesity

An excess of body fat frequently impairs health. More calories are eaten than the body needs. There may be underlying psychological problems.

The Metropolitan Life Insurance Company published in 1983 a Height and Weight Table for Men and Women, ages 25–59, according to frame size. This was based upon a study by the Society of Actuaries and the Association of Life Insurance Medical Directors of America. The table describes the weight at which people live the longest. The insurance company recommends keeping one's weight below average to live longer, although this counsel has been debated. The height is measured in 1-inch heels. Weight is in pounds in indoor clothing. Here is part of the table:

	Men				Women		
Height	Small Frame	Medium Frame	Large Frame	Height	Small Frame	Medium Frame	Large Frame
5'2"	128–134	131–141	138–150	5'2"	108–121	118–132	128–143
5'3"	130–136	133–143	140–153	5'3"	111–124	121–135	131–147
5'4"	132–138	135–145	142–156	5'4"	114–127	124–138	134–151
5'5"	134–140	137–148	144–160	5'5"	117–130	127–141	137–155
5'6"	136–142	139–151	146–164	5'6"	120–133	130–144	140–159
5'7"	138–145	142–154	149–168	5'7"	123–136	133–147	143–163
5'8"	140–148	145–157	152–172	5'8"	126–139	136–150	146–167
5'9"	142–151	148–160	155–176	5'9"	129–142	139–153	149–170
5'10"	144–154	151–163	158–180	5'10"	132–145	142–156	152–173
5'11"	146–157	154–166	161–184	5'11"	135–148	145–159	155–176
6'0"	149–160	157–170	164–188	6'0"	138–151	148–162	158–179

Some experts think these weights are too restrictive for those in their fifties and sixties.

Tips on Dieting

(1) Have regular balanced meals, three times a day.
(2) Make a list before shopping and only buy what is on the list.
(3) Eat smaller portions served on a small plate.
(4) Exercise daily.
(5) Eat slowly so you are not finished eating before your lunch companions and have to sit and watch them eat.
(6) Eat fewer sweets, fats, and high-calorie snacks.
(7) Use skim milk.
(8) Broil or bake instead of frying.

Here are some low calorie menus from the U.S. Department of Agriculture's booklet *Eating for Better Health*.

1200 Calories

	Serving size	Calories		Serving size	Calories
BREAKFAST			BREAKFAST		
Orange juice	6 oz	89	Grapefruit	½	55
Melted cheese on	1 oz	105	Low-sugar cereal	1¼ cups	106
shredded wheat	1 biscuit	88	Skim milk	½ cup	43
Beverage			Beverage		
LUNCH			LUNCH		
Vegetable soup	1 cup	48	Tuna-apple salad	½ cup	126
Hamburger, lean	3 oz, cooked	240	Whole-wheat		
French or Italian			crackers	5 crackers	81
bread or roll	1 slice	73	Skim milk	1 cup	86
Skim milk	1 cup	85	Beverage		
DINNER			DINNER		
Baked fish with creole			Bean-cheese		
sauce	1 serving	91	enchiladas	2	472
Rice	½ cup	92	Spinach	½ cup	23
Cooked okra	½ cup	27	Tossed salad	1¼ cups	17
Cucumber			Low-calorie		
spears	½ cup	10	salad dressing	2 tablespoons	14
Fruit	1 med. piece	63	Fresh fruit	1 med. piece	80
Beverage			Beverage		
SNACK			SNACK		
Banana			Fruit and juice		
milkshake	1½ cups	187	gelatin	¾ cup	96
	Total Calories	1198		Total Calories	1199

More active women and men may need more calories. Increase serving sizes or add a slice of bread to meals to reach 1500 calories.

Low Calorie Recipes

VEGETABLE SOUP

3½ cups water
2 beef, chicken, or vegetable bouillon cubes
¼ teaspoon garlic powder
pinch of pepper
1 small onion, chopped

3 large stalks celery, chopped
2 carrots, thinly sliced
⅛ head cabbage, shredded
1 cup canned tomatoes

1. Bring water to a boil and add bouillon cubes, garlic powder, and pepper.
2. Add onions, celery, carrots, and cabbage. Boil gently until vegetables are tender.
3. Add tomatoes. Boil gently just until heated through.

Makes four servings about 1 cup each, with 48 calories per serving.

BAKED FISH WITH CREOLE SAUCE

¾ pound fresh or frozen fillets or
1½ lbs. whole fish
½ small onion, chopped
⅓ small green pepper, thinly sliced

8 oz. can tomato sauce
1 teaspoon chili powder
¼ teaspoon salt
⅛ teaspoon pepper

1. Thaw fish, if frozen.
2. Rinse fish in cool water. Drain well.
3. Preheat oven to 350°F.
4. Place fish in 9-by-9-by-2-inch baking pan.
5. Mix together onion, green pepper, tomato sauce, chili powder, and salt and pepper. Pour over fish.
6. Cover pan and bake until fish flakes easily with fork (20 to 30 minutes for fillets, 30 to 40 minutes for whole fish).

Makes four servings, with 91 calories per serving.

TUNA-APPLE SALAD

6½ or 7 oz. can fish (packed in water)
1 unpeeled diced apple
1 stalk celery, chopped

2 tablespoons mayonnaise
1 tablespoon lemon juice
Lettuce as desired

1. Rinse and drain tuna.
2. Mix tuna and other ingredients, except lettuce, in bowl.
3. Use immediately or chill 1 to 2 hours.
4. Serve on a bed of lettuce leaves.

Makes four servings, about ½ cup each, with 126 calories per serving.

BANANA MILKSHAKE

1 cup milk, made from nonfat dry milk   1 banana

1. Mash banana well, add milk and blend with beater or shake in jar.
2. Serve immediately or refrigerate and serve later.

Makes one serving, about 1½ cups with 187 calories.

FRUIT AND JUICE GELATIN

1 tablespoon unflavored gelatin   1 cup sliced fruit such as
2 cups unsweetened fruit juice (do not use   peaches, pears, apples,
   fresh or frozen pineapple juice; it will   bananas, berries, etc.
   not gel)

1. Mix together ¼ cup juice and gelatin in a bowl.
2. Measure another ¼ cup juice, boil it, then add hot juice to the above mixture and stir until gelatin is dissolved.
3. Add remaining juice and stir.
4. Put in refrigerator to set.
5. After the gelatin begins to set a little, add the sliced fruit and return gelatin to refrigerator until firm.

Suggestions

1 Plan one week's menus, using principles of nutrition.

2 Investigate nutrition programs for the elderly in your community.

financial planning for health care

If a person has been in good health previous to retirement and maintained a healthy lifestyle, good health may continue until advanced age. However, it is important to obtain adequate health insurance coverage to supplement Medicare after retirement. Sometimes it is possible to stay with the health insurance coverage of a former employer. Income is usually reduced on retirement, although a combination of Social Security, private pension and savings can partially replace the monthly paycheck.

We all know that the cost of adequate health care is becoming prohibitive. The Health Insurance Association of America cited the following statistics for their 1984 update, which show just how much health care costs have increased.

Over a five-year span from 1977 to 1982, there was a 97 percent increase in the number of people with dental insurance, health insurance benefit payments increased by 111 percent, and premiums for health insurance increased in cost by 97 percent. While the average length of patient stay in a hospital remained steady at 7.6 days, the average cost to the hospital per patient stay increased by 88 percent.

The ratio of health insurance premiums to disposable personal income increased to 4.57 percent. The growth rate of the gross national product in 1983 was 7.7 percent, whereas the growth rate of national health expenditures was 10.9 percent.

How do your personal consumption expenditures compare with other American consumers? The following table indicates the percentage of your total personal consumption expenditures spent in acquiring different products, according to the U.S. Department of Commerce, 1982 data.

Type of Product	Percent of Total Personal Consumption Expenditure
Food (including alcohol)	19.9
Housing	16.8
Household operation	13.7
Transportation	13.5
Medical care	10.9
Clothing, accessories and jewelry	7.1
Recreation	6.4
Personal business	5.6
Private education and research	1.6
Religious and welfare activities	1.4
Personal care	1.3
Tobacco	1.2
Foreign travel and remittances—net	0.3
Death expenses	0.3
	100.0

Inflation has a serious impact on the elderly. Although Social Security benefits do have cost of living adjustments, Social Security alone is insufficient income for a person to maintain his standard of living after retirement. Private pensions average about $3000 a year and have no cost of living adjustment, since a private company could not afford this. If money is saved at a lower rate of interest than the inflation rate, and then the interest is taxed, the money is losing its value in what it can purchase. The elderly need to find out what aids and discounts are available to them.

Developing a Budget

Energy is a major expense for the elderly. Philadelphia Electric is an example of a company which has developed a program—PE Cares—for elderly or disabled customers. These customers are advised to develop a budget, to find out if they are eligible for aid, in paying their bills.

Budget for a Month

Here is the budget form used by PE customers.

1. List the total number of people in your home.   _____

2. Figure out your total monthly income. (This total income should include Net income from all adults in your home.)

Wages (Take Home Pay)	_____
Unemployment Checks	_____
Social Security	_____
Public Assistance	_____
Disability	_____
Pension	_____
Food Stamps	_____
Other (Child Support, Alimony)	_____
TOTAL INCOME	$ _____

3. List all Monthly EXPENSES

Rent or Mortgage (incl. real estate taxes)	_____
Telephone	_____
Gas	_____
Electric	_____
Fuel Heating	_____
Water/Sewer	_____
Food	_____
Cleaning Supplies	_____
Laundry	_____
Clothes	_____
Medical	_____
School	_____
Insurance	_____
Transportation	_____
Personal Items	_____
Monthly Time Payments (loans, charge accounts, layaways, etc.)	_____
Other	_____
TOTAL EXPENSES	$ _____

The booklet goes on to explain various programs for which the elderly may qualify, and guidelines to determine if you are eligible. An example would be the Low-Income Home Energy Assistance Program. When you go to apply, take the following items with you:

(1) Your and your spouse's Social Security numbers

(2) Proof of your total household income

(3) Papers confirming legal alien status

(4) The name and address of your heating supplier

(5) Your heating account number, if you have one

(6) Current fuel bill

(7) Statement from landlord (or lease) indicating that heating charges are included in the rental payment

The guidelines for eligibility change, so it is necessary to contact your energy company and obtain the current guidelines. The current information of PE used the following criteria:

Household Size	Yearly Income
1	$7,875 and under
2	10,575

For each additional person add $2700.

Obtaining Financial Assistance

Food Stamps

You may have a job, own your own home, a car, and have total resources up to $1500 and still be eligible for food stamps. If two people—one over sixty—live in your household, the current limit is $3000. Since the criteria for eligibility change, contact your local Department of Public Welfare, or local County Board of Assistance, to find out if you qualify. Here is an example of what level of income qualifies for food stamps at the time this book was written.

Household Size	Monthly Income
1	$569
2	764

For each additional person add $195. When you apply, take the following items with you:

(1) Proof of everyone's income in your household

(2) Proof of cost for rent or mortgage payments, taxes, insurance, telephone, water and utility bills

(3) Bankbooks and/or other papers that show any savings or assets

(4) Proof of alien status of all household members who are not citizens

(5) Identification—Social Security cards for all household members, driver's license, car registrations, birth certificates, marriage license, and case numbers for any kind of public assistance you may be receiving or have received in the past

Medicaid

The Illinois Department of Public Aid provided me with information about its Medicaid green card, which helps pay for medical care, drugs and supplies. A private insurance deductible is the amount of expense you must incur before the insurance will pay for all or part of the rest. Medicaid has a deductible which is called a "spend-down." After you have incurred expenses equal to your spend down, then Medicaid will assist you. The amount of spend-down varies, depending on monthly income.

You apply for Medicaid for six months at a time. Medical care bills during this six-month period are used as evidence of meeting the requirements for spend-down. The bills can come from all people for whom you are legally responsible, such as spouse and children. When you first apply, you can use old unpaid medical bills toward your spend-down. You become eligible on the day that your medical bills show that you meet your spend-down, through the last day of the same month. Sometimes, you would be better off to tell your caseworker that since you met eligibility late in February, you would rather have her keep your bills and use them to obtain a green card for you for the month of March, so that you would have a card for the whole month. If you are turned down for a Medicaid green card, try again later, since criteria for eligibility change.

You have probably heard about elderly people living together instead of marrying in order to safeguard pension income during retirement. Some older people are now divorcing to avoid losing all their assets and savings, paying for nursing home care. The husband divorces his wife, who has Alzheimer's disease and has not yet been declared incompetent. He makes a financial settlement on her, and when that money has gone to pay the nursing home bills, she is eligible for Medicaid to pay for the nursing home. He is able to retain some of the family assets.

Divorce is a very complicated matter, and a lawyer should be consulted before considering divorce, since there may be unforeseen complications. Even if the husband loves his former wife and continues to visit her, he still feels guilty about divorcing her, and does not want people to find out about the divorce. Other options, such as Adult Day Care, should be explored before considering such a desperate step.

Medicare

In 1983, Medicare began using a new system of paying most hospitals. Under the Prospective Payment System hospitals now are paid fixed amounts based on the principal diagnosis for each Medicare hospital stay. In some cases, the Medicare payment will be more than the hospital's costs; in other cases, the payment will be less than the hospital's costs. In special cases, where costs for necessary care are unusually high, or the length of stay is unusually long, the hospital receives additional payment.

Medicare does not determine the length of your stay in the hospital or the extent of care you receive. The law requires hospitals to accept Medicare payments as payment in full, and hospitals are prohibited from billing the Medicare patient for anything other than applicable deductible and coinsurance amounts, plus any amounts due for noncovered items or services.

When you are a hospital inpatient, Medicare hospital insurance can help pay for inpatient hospital care, if all of the following four conditions are met:

(1) A doctor prescribes inpatient hospital care for treatment of your illness or injury.

(2) You require the kind of care that can only be provided in a hospital.

(3) The hospital is participating in Medicare.

(4) The Utilization Review Committee of the hospital or a Peer Review Organization does not disapprove your stay.

Hospital insurance can help pay for up to ninety days of medically necessary inpatient hospital care in each benefit period.

During 1986, from the first day through the sixtieth day in each benefit period, hospital insurance pays for all covered services, except the first $492. This is called the hospital insurance deductible. The hospital may charge you the deductible only for your first admission in each benefit period. If you are discharged and then readmitted before the benefit periods ends, you do not have to pay the deductible again.

From the sixty-first through the ninetieth day in a benefit period, hospital insurance pays for all covered services except for $123 a day. The hospital may charge you for the $123 a day. You also have sixty reserve days past the ninety days, if you are still hospitalized. These days are for one time only—not renewable. For each reserve day, you pay $246/day and Medicare pays the rest.

Medical Insurance

Your Medicare medical insurance can help pay for:

- doctors' services
- outpatient hospital care
- outpatient physical therapy and speech pathology services
- home health care
- many other health services and supplies which are not covered by Medicare hospital insurance

There is a basic payment rule under medical insurance. After you have $75 in approved charges for covered medical expenses in 1986, medical insurance generally will pay eighty percent of the approved charges for any additional covered services you receive during the rest of the year. You are responsible for the remaining twenty percent. The first $75 in covered expenses is called the medical insurance deductible.

Medicare medical insurance payments are not based on your doctor's or supplier's current charges. They are based on what the law defines as "reasonable charges"—the amounts approved by the Medicare carrier. Because of the way the approved amounts are determined and because of high rates of inflation in medical care prices, the charges approved are often less than the actual charges billed by doctors and suppliers.

Selected outpatient hospital services are partially paid for by Medicare:

- services in an emergency room or outpatient clinic
- laboratory tests billed by the hospital
- x-rays and other radiology services billed by the hospital
- medical supplies such as splints and casts
- drugs and biologicals which cannot be self-administered
- blood transfusions furnished to you as an outpatient

Some outpatient hospital services are not paid for by Medicare.

- routine physical examinations and tests directly related to such examinations

- eye or ear examinations to prescribe or fit eyeglasses or hearing aids
- immunizations (except pneumococcal vaccinations or immunizations required because of an injury or immediate risk of infection)
- routine foot care

When buying supplementary insurance investigate the options available. Usually an insurance policy which covers every dollar not paid by Medicare would be too expensive. The American Association of Retired Persons (AARP) has a booklet, *More Health for Your Dollar: An Older Person's Guide to HMOs*. Health maintenance organizations charge a fixed rate to keep you healthy. If you are sick, your monthly fee does not increase. For more information about Medicare, go to your local Social Security office and request an up-to-date copy of *Your Medicare Handbook*.

Finding Employment

Some people cannot afford to retire, or they miss the social interaction involved in working. If it is not possible to remain at their present jobs, part-time employment or a different type of work may bring in enough money to balance income and expenses.

Jean Cowles, Executive Director, informed me about the Wichita, Kansas, Senior Employment Program:

We believe our program promotes independence in the following ways:

(1) Job Seeking Skills Training—Skills training workshop is geared to teaching clients resume writing skills, interviewing skills, identifying employment goals and skills that make these goals appropriate, building self-esteem. The program goal is to encourage proficiency and independence in the job search.

(2) Business and Industry Referrals—Matching employment opportunities with client skills, referrals to unsubsidized, paid employment.

(3) In-Home Service—A majority of employers seeking home employees for companion care, housekeeping, yard-work, minor home repair, etc., are themselves older. The Senior Employment Program client obtains paid employment and the older employer secures the assistance needed to maintain independent living arrangements in the community at large.

Data on program placements are found in the following table.

Senior Employment Program FY 85 10/1/84 to 9/30/85

	In-Home	Projects with Industry
Employer Requests	1,055	348
Employers Contacted		581
Total Persons Placed	248	208
Permanent		
Part-time		101
Full-time		66
Temporary		
Part-time	239	35
Full-time	19	6
Type of Job:		
Aircraft		7
Carpenter	8	
Child Care	3	
Cleaning/Housekeeping	84	
Companion Care		
Night Support	14	
Day	83	
Live-In	32	
Construction		16
Custodial/Maintenance		12
Driving/Delivery	10	26
Food Service		13
General Office/Secretarial		51
Hotel/Motel		3
Minor Home Repair	71	
Painting	12	
Sales Clerk		25
Yard Work	82	
Other	20	55
TOTAL	419	208

Ellen Sax is the National Director of Projects with Industry. She stated:

The purpose of Aging in America, Projects with Industry, is to assist older and older disabled persons to obtain employment and thereby attain independence. We do this by providing our clients with:

(1) Vocational counseling to help them assess and better understand their skills and abilities.

(2) Financial counseling to understand the job market and how to meet their financial requirements.

(3) Training in how to market themselves. While this is difficult for people of all ages, often an older person has never had to interview for a position (promoted within the company due to track record). Selling one's skills and abilities requires practice.

(4) Emotional support. Job hunting can be one of the most frustrating, disheartening full-time jobs around.

(5) Placement assistance. We work with a growing number of companies who seek mature, reliable employees, and we are often able to match their requirements with our job candidates.

Mr. D. is a seventy-three-year-old male with disabilities including a congenital hearing impairment and arthritis. He was referred to AIA/PWI by the Office of Vocational Rehabilitation after having been retired for five years. Mr. D. related a twenty-year employment history, in the field of auto mechanics, but because of the physical demands could not return to that field. Due to his restlessness in remaining home, Mr. D. was anxious to return to the labor force. Since Mr. D. is unable to use the telephone, it was necessary for him to learn "cold calling" employers through training. During the second week of training, Mr. D. was sent to a company for a position involving light maintenance. Mr. D. was hired and after three years is continuing to do well.

The Kansas City, Missouri Shepherd's Center grew out of the concern of a pastor of a religious congregation to find a way to serve more effectively the older people in his parish. Now there are sixty-two centers, run *by* the elderly as well as for the elderly. Support of each center comes from churches and synagogues in the local area.

A center has four cardinal characteristics:

(1) It is based upon the idea that older people are a potential resource for the enrichment of the life of the community rather than a social problem to be solved. Older people are seen as possessing skills, experience, wisdom, matured judgment, which can be called upon for service, and it is believed that fulfillment in the later life requires that persons be allowed to assume significant social roles, which they can enjoy and the community can appreciate.

(2) It is based upon the idea that older people must assume responsibility for their own lives and for the development of programs affecting them as persons and the community as a whole.

(3) It is based upon the concept of community and of neighborhood, in which people care for each other, because they care about each other.

(4) It seeks, solicits, and depends upon the support and sponsorship of the religious congregations within the neighborhood it serves. Religious congregations can provide the undergirding symbols and system of values, which enable persons to find meaning and purpose for their lives. The centers try to enable persons and congregations to draw upon and share those insights and values, which they share in common, without vitiating particular traditions.

The centers see the use of volunteers primarily as a way of enabling persons to invest their time and talents in meaningful and self-fulfilling ways. However, because of the mobilization of self-help and volunteer service, communities can do much more for themselves than if everything had to be paid for.

Here is an example of how the centers work—the handyman program:

> In 1972, a dedicated meals on wheels volunteer and retired painter raised his concern that so many homes of the meal recipients were in need of repair, yet most of the recipients were elderly, on fixed incomes, and unable to make repairs. When asked what he (as an older volunteer) thought could be done, he proposed the practical solution of calling a group of recently retired painters, carpenters, plumbers, and similarly skilled retirees, who might consider teaming up to provide service to older persons, whose homes were in need of minor repairs. The handymen keep their skills and their sense of pride alive, while in many cases supplementing an otherwise fixed income through the small $5.00/hour fee. It serves those who need minor repairs, at prices they can afford, while keeping the skilled workman alive to his own abilities and providing him with the assurance of his continuing value to others and the community.

Dianne Cantrell, Executive Director, and Kathleen Jackson, Director, provided details about the state of Indiana's Older Worker Employment Program. The program determines the job-seeker's marketable skills, training needs, and required supportive services. Potential employers are contacted through a variety of methods: networking, telephone contacts, advertisements, public service announcements, community presentations, and presentations to individual employers. His "Job Club" for the older job seeker is described as follows:

> Upon entering the Job Club, specific techniques are further enhanced and built upon: interviewing skills, networking, employer expectations, developing job leads, and telephone techniques. Positive results from the Job Club include the sharing of job leads, peer counseling, and personality and human relations development.

Negative attitudes become positive; new members are "pounced on" for expressing negative feelings. An example of the positiveness of the Job Club experience came when a stranger attended the Job Club. When it was determined that the stranger was attending the wrong meeting, the man stayed anyhow. He is now a volunteer, making presentations within the community.

Subsidized placements are for specific time periods. Length and subsidy as indicated by the specific situation. A subsidized placement was made in a small branch store, enabling the store to expand business hours. The person placed was excellent in sales, which increased sales, requiring additional sales help. Another person was hired through the program. The new branch manager is now in contention for a prize offered by the company.

Some social services are needed to remove barriers to employment of specific individuals. Transportation, better clothes, counselling, and/or services are provided or linked. One woman was self-conscious of her appearance. The solution was to have her attend a beauty college, to alter her make-up and hair and to suggest different attire.

The National Caucus and Center on Black Aged, Older Workers' Training Program, is described by Samuel Simmons, its president, as follows: "The unique feature of this program is that we are taking low-income people with average incomes of $3400 per year and enabling them to become totally independent of government subsidies." The following is from the program's literature.

The purpose of this program is to provide a training and employment program for older workers and senior retirees that prepares them for professional, competitive management positions in the housing industry. All participants are simultaneously enrolled in the American Association of Retired Persons Title V Senior Employment Program, receiving minimum wages subsidies ($3.35 per hour) twenty hours per week for the entire length of the program, which consists of:

- twelve weeks, classroom learning: process and content; site visits
- eight weeks, on-the-job training at host housing agencies, including individual portfolio development
- five weeks, industry certification preparation
- twelve weeks, follow-up, job placement—job counseling, including job readiness and resume development
- twenty-four weeks, follow-up on-site technical assistance re: permanent jobs

Curriculum Content—Nine key areas:

(1) Occupancy, including certification and recertification
(2) Fundamental management considerations, including supervisory skills

(3) Maintenance, including preventive, routine and emergency, scheduling and unit inspections

(4) Non-shelter services

(5) Personnel and staffing

(6) Budgeting and recordkeeping

(7) Security

(8) Resident relations

(9) Administration of congregate services including institutional food, service, transportation and homemaking

Curriculum Process—Participants also improve:

- communication skills
- conflict resolution
- interpersonal skills
- management skills
- team building
- problem-solving
- experiential learning
- management reviews
- site visits

Profile—Recent District of Columbia Pilot Program

- 25 enrollees—8 drop-outs or terminations due to illness, family problems or career change
- 17 graduates, 13 women, 4 men
- age range 55–84
- first permanent job placement: Resident Manager of a 270-unit apartment complex. NCBA graduate went from subsidized income of $3532 to an unsubsidized $15,000 per year plus a two-bedroom apartment, a 400% increase of income.

Major Outcome of Tampa/St. Petersburg Program

- minimum wage subsidies for all participants during training
- competitive permanent job placement
- provision of adequate skills and knowledge
- follow-up technical assistance re: on-site problems
- three major NCBA publications
- an easily replicated career development system
- a career development system which is immediately adaptable to other areas

Mrs. Jean Brown explained how Bed and Breakfast International works:

The first person whose life was changed was mine! The idea originated as a means of supplementing my husband's retirement income. I was tired of teaching. All my friends had spare rooms because the kids had gone to college; we were Bed and Breakfast European travellers; and I knew from the minute I thought of it that it would work. Plenty of people said, "You aren't going to put strangers into American homes! It could work in Europe, but not here." Ten thousand guests later, and not a washrag has been stolen. This is at least partly due to the way we operate.

There are now 160 women, and some men running their own B & B reservation services all over the country. I guess that the gratification this has given to me has been greater than the negative effects of self-employment, the time demands that keep me from getting out and hiking with my husband, and that have tied him to the house also, the stress of competing and starting a business from scratch without business training, and the strain of relating to so many people and trying to put the right people in the right place.

My first host story concerns a widow in her late 70s, whose husband had been an artist. Her home showed the taste of their interests, but it was beginning to be run down and neglected. She had been active in many organizations, in fact, she also was a nurse. However, it gets harder to get yourself out as you get older, and you don't try as hard. Her first guests were an English couple being taken around by their daughter, an airline stewardess. She really cleaned up the house, and for months after they left, the daughter invited her into downtown San Francisco to have lunch with her, when she flew into San Francisco. The widow used to phone me after every guest to tell me about them, and to discuss new things she was buying for her home in order to make them more comfortable. Talk about turning a life around.

But you see this has happened to every woman I work with. Our hosts get hooked on it, and never leave. I think of one lady who was just the opposite of the first: a woman well-off financially with a luxurious home, who was very wary of the whole thing. She didn't want this kind of guest, and she wasn't going to let them do this and that, and they couldn't expect her to wait on them, on and on. Well she is actually a lonely and insecure person, who wants people to like her, so she didn't do a bad job, grudging though it was. People did enjoy her extraordinary location and home, and responded well to her with thank you notes to her and us. This really pleased her and she began to relax and to give more to people and she is really into it now.

Suggestions

1 Find out what your private health insurance and/or Medicare will cover.

2 Plan for the future based on your analysis of your potential or actual health care needs.

3 Investigate the following resources:

Hospital Care: Hill-Burton Hospital Free Care (800)638-0742, (800)492-0359 in Maryland, provides information on hospitals participating in the Hill-Burton Hospital Free Care Program. A service of the Bureau of Health Maintenance Organizations and Resources Development, U.S. Department of Health and Human Services.

Income Tax: Federal Internal Revenue Service for TDD Users (800)428-4732, (800)382-4095 in Indiana, answers questions on federal income tax, including questions on medical deductions for the cost of telecommunications devices for the deaf (TDDs), hearing aids, trained hearing-ear dogs. Accepts orders for the free publication *Tax Information for Handicapped and Disabled Individuals* and other free IRS publications.

Insurance: American Council of Life Insurance, Health Insurance Association of America (800)423-8000, (202)862-4054 in DC, answers general questions about life and health insurance; does not handle complaints regarding insurance claims.

Medicare/Medicaid: Dept. of Health and Human Services Inspector General's Hotline (800)368-5779, (301)579-0724 in Maryland, handles complaints regarding fraud, waste, and abuse of government funds, including Medicare and Medicaid. Assists people who have been overbilled or billed for services not rendered.

adapting to psychosocial changes

Health is defined by the World Health Organization (WHO) as physical, psychological, and social well-being. As people age, it becomes more difficult for them to adapt to psychosocial changes. Intelligence does not decrease rapidly unless the person is ill, but it does take longer for elderly people to process and respond to information. They can learn if given time and if new material is related to previous learning in a meaningful manner. Also, the teacher has to remedy deficits in sight and hearing, or assist the elderly person to compensate for these deficits.

The elderly have a short attention span and a decrease in short-term memory. It is preferable to have frequent teaching sessions spread over several days and reinforced, rather than one long teaching session without any follow-up. Written material as a reference when the teacher is not there is helpful. If the teaching relates to psychomotor skills, such as giving insulin, the elderly person needs opportunities for practice and for giving a return demonstration.

I walked into a patient's room and found a doctor examining her. On the basis that she was not answering his questions, the doctor told his interns that the patient had had a stroke, which interfered with her communication. My nursing student went up to the doctor and told him that the patient's hearing aid battery was not working. The doctor re-examined the patient when she had a new battery and was able to communicate. It is essential to check out all assistive devices for impaired function before making decisions about a person's health status.

Families should acquaint themselves with the factors which can cause psychosocial problems for the elderly. In Washington, DC, the

Downtown Cluster's Geriatric Day Care Center conducted a needs assessment of its older clients. Participants indicated that their needs include medical and non-medical transportation services, older worker employment training programs, case management services, weekend leisure activities, information and referral, family support services, socialization programs, intergenerational programs, canned food programs, home-delivered meals, and friendly caller services.

The Center provided comprehensive social services. Zoila Kohler, Director, told me that these services included:

- individual, family and group counseling, and comprehensive case management
- assistance in obtaining Medicaid, food stamps, energy assistance, Supplementary Security Income, canned foods, social security, and medical transportation
- Family members and caregivers are encouraged to participate in the caregiver's support group at the Center.
- advocacy assistance
- literacy skills training

With all the problems or potential problems it is not surprising that the frail elderly require a variety of services. The Cluster costs $25.79 per person per day. The program is funded through the District of Columbia Office on Aging. Other funding sources include the United Black Fund, Medicare reimbursements, participant contributions, and other grants. A variety of volunteer organizations help with transportation, nutrition, the arts, and recreation. One eighty-three-year-old volunteer is present four days a week to serve lunches to participants.

Theories of Psychological Aging

There are various theories of psychological aging. The disengagement theory suggests that elderly people are ready to reduce their interaction with society and limit themselves to interaction with family members or close friends. The elderly become fatigued sooner than the middle-aged. In contrast, the activity theory suggests that maintaining activity and replacing lost roles with new roles increase life satisfaction.

The exchange theory suggests that older people are in a disadvantaged position in society because they have fewer social resources to exchange. As one might expect, above average income and socioeconomic status are related to increased life satisfaction.

The continuity theory suggests that although challenges change, a person will probably retain the same way of coping with challenges that he used when middle-aged. Also, personality in terms of habits, commitments, and associations will remain close to what it has been when younger. People who have always lived in a city like the availability of activities and services, whereas people who live in the country like the close intrafamily contact and the lower crime rate. People who make a drastic change in their lifestyles after retirement are sometimes very disappointed and return to their old neighborhoods.

Depression

More than nine million people in the U.S. are depressed. Twenty-five percent of elderly suicides are related to persistent depression. Causes of depression include: physical ill-health, socioeconomic disadvantage, loss, stressful life events, and absence of a caring relationship.

Depressed people turn inward and think and talk only of themselves. They feel like a failure. It is important for them to experience success, with something they do well. Depression may be manifested by restlessness, changes in weight, appetite, and sleep patterns. This may be masked by drug and alcohol abuse.

Since the aging process is accompanied by physiologic changes that alter the body's response to both food and drugs, practices of self-medication, over-prescribing and use of two or more drugs can create serious health problems for the elderly. Misuse of alcohol and drugs increases risks to health. When people who are dependent on alcohol attempt to stop drinking, they can develop tremors and insomnia. Continued alcohol abuse may lead to cirrhosis of the liver and weakening of the heart muscle's pumping action and rhythm. Blackouts may occur, with eventual brain damage. Admission to a detoxification center followed by counseling and/or Alcoholics Anonymous may be necessary to save the person's life.

According to a publication of the National Institute on Drug Abuse, women are more likely to go to a doctor with complaints of anxiety, tension, sleeplessness and depression. So they are more likely to receive prescriptions for drugs that affect their mood. Depressant drugs, such as alcohol, tranquilizers, and sleeping pills, make people sleepy and slow down breathing and circulation by depressing the central nervous system.

Here are some danger signals that the National Institute on Drug

Abuse warns that a person taking depressant drugs should watch out for:

- Do those close to you often ask about your drug use? Have they noticed any changes in your moods or behavior?
- Are you defensive if a friend or relative mentions your drug or alcohol use?
- Are you sometimes embarrassed or frightened by your behavior under the influence of drugs or alcohol?
- Have you ever gone to see a new doctor because your regular physician would not prescribe the drug you wanted?
- When you are under pressure or feeling anxious, do you automatically take a tranquilizer or drink or both?
- Do you take drugs more often or for purposes other than those recommended by your doctor?
- Do you mix drugs and alcohol?
- Do you drink or take drugs regularly to help you sleep?
- Do you have to take a pill to get going in the morning?

If you have answered yes to a number of these questions, you may be misusing drugs or alcohol. In your community, drug abuse programs are listed in the Yellow Pages. Community crisis centers and hotlines also provide help. If you have trouble finding help in your community, you may want to contact the state-level agency for drug abuse in your state. A person recoverng from alcohol or drug abuse may need psychotherapy. If depression is a factor, then treatment such as medication, electroconvulsant therapy, environmental and psychotherapy may be necessary.

Sexuality

Elderly men take longer to develop an erection and it subsides more rapidly. There is an increase in the resting period when a person cannot have another erection. Elderly women have less lubrication and the vagina is less elastic. Orgasms are less intensive and of shorter duration.

Emotional problems, fatigue, abuse of alcohol, and antihypertensive drugs can have a negative effect on sexual intercourse, as can certain diseases, such as heart disease, diabetes, and arthritis, depending upon how severe the disease is. Ask a doctor specifically how a disease may affect a person's sexuality.

Elderly men may have a fear of failure. Elderly widows may not be able to find another partner. People who are residents of a nursing home or live with their children may have very little privacy, since society does not accept the sexuality of older people. Remarriage may not be accepted by adult children, if it involves a change in an expected inheritance. Couples may decide to live together instead of remarriage, if remarriage would cause the loss of a widow's private pension or a decrease in benefits.

Promoting Mental Health

Ileane Stone, Director of Social Services, and Michele Koonin, a private consultant, communicated with me about the group work they conducted at St. Paul's Manor and Health Care Center in San Diego, California. They explained that groups that work best with the elderly have the following characteristics:

- constancy of time and place
- selected members
- limited number of sessions
- limited number of group members
- verbal contracts from the members to attend
- confidentiality
- a facilitator who understands and accepts the aging process

Ms. Stone and Ms. Koonin note that:

> Generally, seniors are reluctant to ask for help and do not easily acknowledge their need for mental health services. Groups have been found to be more successful with this population when they are offered in the home environment, are not presented as therapy, and are limited to a certain number of sessions.
>
> <u>Selection of group members</u>—In selecting group members, the following criteria may be valuable:
>
> - clients who may be seen by staff as depressed, assessed by changes in appetite, isolation, staying in their rooms more than usual, non-participation in activities, tearful or angry outbursts
> - clients who self-report any changes in their normal routine, such as sleeping or eating habits
> - clients who have poor personal hygiene, representing a change in their prior habits
> - clients who seek out staff attention on a constant basis
>
> Many clients may self-report feeling 'poorly.' Often this will be done in physical rather than psychological complaints. Staff should be alert to

these kinds of signals from clients. Those clients who are new to the program or the facility are often good candidates for groups, as this may be a difficult transition for them and help can be very valuable. Clients who have suffered recent losses, including spouses, friends, ability to drive, a family who has moved away, or physical illness may also greatly benefit from a supportive group. A very good rule for choosing prospective group members is to look for clients who have had some changes in their lives recently, as changes become more and more difficult to deal with as aging occurs.

Seating arrangement—We have found that the best seating arrangement for the group is a circle which allows each member to see one another and be in close contact with each other and the leaders.

Staff support—It cannot be stressed enough that for a group of seniors to be successful, it must have the support of the agency that is sponsoring it. All staff members must be aware of the group and its importance to group members. This will avoid or minimize double scheduling of activities or possible sabotage by staff members. The support of the group by staff members is a necessary and vital ingredient to the survival of the group. Group leaders should explain its purpose to staff, and schedule meetings at a time that least conflicts with other activities. Other issues to include when planning the group are: record-keeping, confidentiality, the absence or death of a group member.

Sara G. was chosen for the group because of her social isolation, depression and loneliness and lack of a support system. She had created a family in her apartment by collecting muppet dolls. After she became a group member, she disclosed her hobby. The members of the group were so impressed with her creativity in making numerous seasonal changes of wardrobe for the dolls that she was then asked to present them at an open house display.

Sara G. was so thrilled at this recognition of her talents that she began to make many new friends. She was able to keep her independence and elevate her self-worth by sharing with others and receiving praise in return. She has become fond of Kahlua, and has 'dog sat' for him on numerous occasions, giving him the love she had previously given only to her dolls. She also shares her times of 'dog sitting' with other group members by taking him to their apartments and bringing him to the more frail residents in the Health Care Center. She has found a family within the group and there is a very close, bonding relationship among the members.

Madeline B. is an extremely shy, reserved lady, eighty-six years of age, who is often labeled unfriendly and a snob. She is always well-groomed and in the past has been the president of many women's clubs. She was asked to join the group because of depression. After a few sessions, she began to share stories about her past life, enthralling the group, as she is an excellent storyteller. Confidentiality affords her the opportunity to unload on the group, because it stays only within the group. She receives affection from the group members, and has even learned to be somewhat assertive with others instead of holding in her anger, or retreating to her apartment.

One important group session involved role playing about 'insideness in the dining room.' Madeline took one of the key roles in which she was rebuffed by others who would not let her sit with them at their table. The group then problem-solved, to help her cope with the situation. Madeline took their suggestions and used them in the actual dining room setting, instead of having her meals alone in her room. She maintained her independence by asserting herself, and feeling good about what she had done. Her self-esteem was greatly elevated as a result of sharing her feelings and receiving feedback from others. She is no longer the victim, but the victor.

Suggestion

1 Identify how you could help someone with depression.

stress

What is stress? One definition is that stress is any psychophysiologic response to a stimulus event we perceive as threatening. This response prepares the person for "fight-or-flight." There is an increase in muscle tension, heart rate, respiration and blood pressure, and a decrease in saliva. There is an elevation in sodium retention, serum glucose and hydrochloric acid.

A stressor is a factor with the potential to cause stress. Threats may be physical: damage to the body, weather, and diet; or psychological: decrease in self-esteem, and threats relating to self-concept; or sociological: unemployment, death of a spouse. Older people are more sensitive to stress than young people. The short-term effects of stress on the heart and muscles are better understood than the long-term effects, such as hypertension.

People respond differently to stress at different times. Also, they respond differently to anticipated stress than to unanticipated stress. Elderly people who live in a high crime rate neighborhood may live in constant fear and stress, even if they are never the actual victim of a crime. Activities to reduce stress—smoking, drinking, pills—may have a negative effect on the person's health.

Reactions to Stress

Stress reaction as described by physiologist Hans Selye is a three phase process:

PHASE 1: Alarm reaction—The body shows the changes characteristic of the first exposure to a stressor. At the same time, its resistance is diminished and, if the stressor is sufficiently strong (severe burns, extremes of temperature), death may result.

PHASE 2: Stage of resistance—Resistance ensues if continued exposure to the stressor is compatible with adaptation. The bodily signs characteristic of the alarm reaction have virtually disappeared, and resistance rises above normal.

PHASE 3: Stage of exhaustion—Following long-continued exposure to the same stressor, to which the body had become adjusted, eventually adaptation energy is exhausted. The signs of the alarm reaction reappear, but now they are irreversible, and the individual dies.

A stressor is perceived as a threat. The person has an emotional and physiological arousal. If the stress is long lasting and the person does not fight or run away, stress products are not used up, and break down the body, resulting in disease.

Perception is the process which attaches meaning to and interprets events. It can be influenced by the state of a person's physical health, or psychosocial past experiences. Elderly people have diminished effectiveness of sensory reception, and they also take a longer time for the brain to process and interpret information.

Sensation is the term applied to what occurs each time a receptor organ is stimulated. Sensory adaptation has an effect on individual perception. For example, when you leave the house at night, it is difficult to see. In a few minutes your eyes adapt to the darkness, so that you can see better. On the other hand, musicians exposed for long periods of time to loud rock music lose part of the sensitivity of their hearing.

Perception of a stressor as a threat initiates the "fight-or-flight" response of stress. However, through selective awareness, you can deliberately focus on the positive points of a situation, so that it will not be perceived as a threat.

Some stress may be beneficial and lead to improved productivity. Unless suitably managed, however, stress may contribute to physical and psychological problems, such as depression, fatigue, obesity, coronary heart disease, suicide, or violence. Suicide and homicide are the causes of more than 50,000 deaths annually. The elderly and the economically disadvantaged appear more vulnerable to stress.

How does stress manifest itself in the different body systems? In the cardiovascular system, the stress hormones norepinephrine and epinephrine increase the constriction of the blood vessels in the limbs. If this constriction is present, then there is increased pressure on the vessel walls due to the blood being pumped through a vessel of decreased diameter. These hormones also increase the heart rate and cardiac output. Other hormones act to retain fluid in the body, which increases the blood volume.

In the gastrointestinal system, saliva is decreased. That is why you have a dry mouth and difficulty in swallowing, when under stress. The smooth muscle of the esophagus, stomach, and intestine has a coordinated rhythmic peristalsis, which is disrupted by stress. Stomach peristalsis is slowed down while the secretion of hydrochloric acid is increased, which can cause ulcers. Stress can either slow down the small intestine, causing constipation, or speed it up, causing diarrhea.

Skeletal muscles contract (also known as bracing) due to tension and the "fight-or-flight" response. This contraction leads to a decreased oxygen and blood supply, which leads to pain, soreness, and fatigue. The skeletal muscles can store tension through bracing. That is the rationale for progressive relaxation as a technique, since it is not possible for the mind to be full of tension if the muscles in the body are deliberately relaxed.

Stress and Disease

Psychogenic disease is a physical disease caused by emotional stress, such as asthma, hypertension, ulcers. There is no microorganism invasion. The mind changes the physiology so that parts of the body break down. Psychosomatic disease occurs when the mind increases the body's susceptibility to disease-causing microorganisms. Stress decreases the number of lymphocytes available to fight infection. Stress also increases the body's susceptibility to degenerative process. Examples include cancer or rheumatoid disease.

Psychogenic Asthma

In asthma, there is an allergy defense mechanism involved. Following an invasion by some foreign substance (antigen), which should not be in the respiratory system, the body produces antibodies to neutralize or destroy the antigen. These antibodies then stimulate the release of chemicals, such as histamine, which swells mucous membranes, constricts air passages, increases mucus to keep foreign substances out or to trap the foreign substances in the mucus. Breathing may become difficult. An antihistamine medication helps. Normally, T lymphocytes destroy foreign substances in the blood, but when the person is stressed, the effectiveness of the immune system is diminished.

Hypertension

Ninety percent of hypertension cases are of unknown origin—primary hypertension. Ten percent are due to kidney disease or another disease—referred to as secondary hypertension. If the underlying cause can be treated, then secondary hypertension will disappear.

Blood pressure is the amount of pressure exerted on the walls of arteries as blood circulates through. Systolic is the amount of pressure exerted when the heart is pumping, while diastolic is the amount of pressure exerted when the heart is resting. Hypertension is a psychogenic disease. The World Health Organization defines hypertension as a blood pressure above 140 systolic and/or above 90 diastolic.

Twenty percent of adults suffer from sustained high blood pressure. Factors responsible for elevated blood pressure due to stress are:

(1) Increased peripheral resistance—This is the term used to describe the constriction of the blood vessels in the limbs, caused by the release of norepinephrine and epinephrine from the adrenal gland. The heart has to pump harder to circulate blood through constricted vessels.

(2) Increased blood volume—The hormones vasopressin and oxytocin from the pituitary gland make the blood vessels absorb more fluid into the bloodstream. The hormone aldosterone, from the adrenal gland, increases the retention of sodium and water, and decreases urine output.

(3) Cardiac output—This measurement is equal to the heart rate times the stroke volume. Since epinephrine and norepinephrine increase the heart rate and stroke volume, this increases the cardiac output, which leads to a higher blood pressure.

Blood pressure screening is necessary, since early hypertension is asymptomatic. Later signs and symptoms include headache, tiredness, and nose bleed. Hypertension has potential serious complications. A person can have a heart attack or heart failure, when trying to pump against increased peripheral resistance. Elevated blood pressure can lead to a ruptured cerebral blood vessel causing a stroke.

The treatment of hypertension is difficult because the person doesn't feel sick and often doesn't comply with treatment. The major goal is to lower the blood pressure gradually to about 160/95 or whatever the doctor considers to be appropriate. If the blood pressure were abruptly lowered in an elderly person to a low level, the pressure might not be high enough to circulate blood to the brain.

The management of hypertension which is only slightly elevated would include decreasing weight if obese, participation in a prescribed exercise program, and remaining on a low fat, low sodium, low calorie diet if necessary. An obese person needs more blood vessels than normal to provide nourishment to the tissues, which means the heart has to work harder. A low sodium diet will not retain as much water in the blood circulation, which will help decrease the blood pressure.

If these conservative measures do not work, then diuretic drugs which increase urine output and decrease blood volume are tried. Should the blood pressure still be elevated, then other more potent drugs, which decrease the constriction of the blood vessels, are prescribed. The problem is that more potent drugs have more side effects. For example, some of them cause impotence, and people may not take them as prescribed because of this side effect.

Rheumatoid Arthritis

Psychosomatic rheumatoid arthritis is a disease manifested by inflammation and swelling due to a proliferation of synovial membrane, in various body joints. The cause is unknown. One hypothesis is that there are bacteria in the synovial membrane, which lines joints. Antibodies produced to fight these bacteria attack the body's own cells. A blood protein called the rheumatoid factor has been found in fifty percent of people with rheumatoid arthritis. The role this blood protein plays in the disease has not been proved yet. There is evidence that people with rheumatoid arthritis have a personality type which shows more depression and perfectionist tendencies than normal. However, when someone has a chronic disease, it is not always possible to determine whether the personality was a factor causing the disease, or the depression is a result of having difficulty coping with a chronic illness.

Biological Rhythms

Stress can interfere with the regularity of biological rhythms. For example, the glucocorticoid hormones have a daily pattern of secretion, possibly synchronized by light. During sleep, the level of these hormones in the urine and blood decreases. In the early morning, it reaches its highest level, drops around 10 a.m., rises gradually until 2 p.m., then declines until 10 p.m. Flying long distances or shift work can desynchronize this rhythm.

The glucocorticoid hormones have an effect on carbohydrate and protein metabolism. They also protect the body from the effects of stress, through their anti-inflammatory effect. Normally, increased stress should stimulate increased secretion of glucocorticoid. However, if the rhythm has been desynchronized, the hormone levels may be lower during the day than they should be. Research has shown that if the adrenal gland cannot produce enough glucocorticoids to combat stress, the person may die.

The sleep time cycle is affected by age. More sleep time is needed in infancy and childhood. Also, the number of awakenings is highest in infancy. Adults sleep from six to nine hours. There is a wide variety of sleep needs.

Sleep is made up of rapid eye movement (REM) sleep, and quiet, non-REM sleep. One goes through cycles of non-REM sleep and REM sleep, about five times a night, with each cycle lasting about ninety minutes. Shift workers get less sleep than others and complain more about fatigue, psychological problems, and digestive problems.

The National Association of Bedding Manufacturers publishes a guide, *Good Night, America: A Guide to Better Sleep*. The booklet is available for $1.50, from the Better Sleep Council, a nonprofit educational organization. Their address is P.O. Box 275, Burtonsville, Maryland, 20866. Here are some tips from *Good Night*.

Environment is an important factor in facilitating sleep. Temperature in the sixties, quiet room, and darkened room is preferable for sleep. Insomnia is a broad term which can mean different specific problems: the person cannot fall asleep within an hour; cannot get six hours of sleep; cannot sleep through the night without long periods of wakefulness. The following actions may help.

(1) Progressive Muscle Relaxation—This involves alternate tensing and relaxation of muscles. Focus on one group at a time. Tense them tightly for five to seven seconds, then release them for fifteen to twenty seconds and repeat with other muscle groups. Tell yourself as you relax the muscles in your arms and legs that you can feel your arm or leg becoming heavy and warm. Relaxing your muscles will relax your mind so you can sleep.

(2) Transcendental Meditation—This involves concentrating on one's breathing in and out, and counting "one" as you breathe out. Other thoughts that come into your mind are dismissed. Meditating for

twenty minutes two times a day promotes mental relaxation. People who are interested in transcendental meditation have the opportunity to study the philosophy behind the practice. They would also be given their own mantra, which is a phrase to use when concentrating on your breathing, instead of just counting "one." There are various centers throughout the U.S. People do not have to change their religious practices to use this technique.

(3) Snacks rich in L-tryptophan—This amino acid has been described as nature's sleeping pill. It is found in milk, eggs, tuna fish, cottage cheese, and chicken.

Sleeping pills lose their effectiveness with regular use and can cause side effects, such as drowsiness during the day. Occasional use of two aspirin at night can promote sleep. Unfortunately, people may have gastric bleeding if they take aspirin regularly. Elderly people need less sleep. They should avoid daytime naps and exercise daily. If you have a sleep problem, you can obtain a list of accredited sleep disorder centers from the Association of Sleep Disorders Centers, P.O. Box 2604, Del Mar, California 92014, Attention: Merrill Mitler, Ph.D.

Here is a quiz from *Good Night*.

1. *Are you usually sleepy at bedtime?*

   Yes, very   Moderately   No, not at all

2. *Do you follow a sleep ritual before getting into bed?*

   Yes, always   Usually   Rarely   Never

3. *Rate your typical bedtime mood on a scale of one to ten.*

                    1 2 3 4 5 6 7 8 9 10

   Anxious   Tense   Relaxed

4. *What time do you usually go to bed?*

5. *Do you go to bed at a different time during the weekend?*

6. *How long does it take you to fall asleep on weeknights? Weekends?*

7. *Do you awaken in the night? How often? For how long?*

8. *What do you do when you wake up in the night or too early in the morning?*

9. *What time do you usually wake up?*

10. *What time do you get out of bed on weekdays? Weekends?*

11. *Rate your typical morning energy level.*

                    1 2 3 4 5 6 7 8 9 10

   Extremely sleepy   Groggy   Alert

12. *Do you feel very drowsy during the day? Any particular time?*

13. Do you nap during the day? How often? For how long?

14. How many hours do you typically spend sleeping in a 24 hour period?

15. Are you dissatisfied with how long or well you sleep?

16. When was the last time you slept satisfactorily?

17. Do you use sleeping pills?

Never   Occasionally   Regularly

18. Do you use large amounts of stimulants (coffee, cigarettes, tea, drugs)?

19. Do you take any medication regularly?

20. If your sleep set is at least 8 to 10 years old, have you done a bed check recently?

If you perceive that your answers to the quiz indicate a problem, see your family doctor.

Blue Cross and Blue Shield has a booklet, *Stress*, which they will send you. They suggest the following strategies for elderly people to cope with stress:

(1) Conserve your energy. Fight for important things, but dismiss unimportant matters.

(2) Develop a network of friends.

(3) Maintain hope and a positive attitude.

(4) Try to anticipate future stressors and plan to handle them.

Suggestions

1 Identify symptoms of stress.

2 Develop a plan for coping with stress.

the arts and aging

In 1973, the National Council developed a program, the National Center on Arts and the Aging. This program was in response to the interest displayed by the elderly in artistic expression and appreciation. With their longer life expectancy, people's participation in creative activities promotes even greater emotional well-being and more meaning in life.

Katie Gibson, Arts Coordinator of the Iowa Arts Council, described the goals of the group as follows:

> We intend to provide a service for elderly Iowans that will enable them to adjust better to the trauma and stress that often accompany:
>
> (1) The transition from full employment to retirement
> (2) The transition from independent living to a nursing home situation
> (3) The loss of spouse, friends, and interest in life
>
> Although the years from age sixty on are often wrought with stress, change and losses (job, spouses, friends) little attention is given to their mental and emotional needs, and instead, only to economic and physical needs. Yet, caring for mental/emotional needs might alleviate or lessen economic needs by keeping older people contentedly in their home situation rather than moving them to a more costly nursing/retirement home because of depression caused by a feeling of isolation and loss of confidence.
>
> The Iowa Arts Council provides professional artists to conduct participatory creative arts programs at sites accessible to the elderly, and at hours convenient for them. The artists teach basic techniques. The discipline may be in a visual art (painting, pottery, or photography), a performing art (music, drama or dance/movement) or a literary art (poetry

or creative writing). Students develop their own individual work as well as one 'group piece' that the class presents as a gift to their community. The group gift varies from art exhibitions to anthologies or music/drama productions, and is a gala affair with local publicity.

The Program Coordinator arranges community involvement by:

(1) Encouraging middle-aged community people to take part in classes with those sixty and over

(2) Soliciting volunteers to assist with classes

(3) Soliciting local artists to continue the arts activity on a volunteer basis when funding is exhausted

(4) Inviting school children to visit classes as well as the final exhibit or performance

Objectives of an Arts Program

The arts program was intended to:

- reverse negative attitudes about aging, held by the elderly themselves, staff workers, school children and the community at large
- offer the elderly a stimulating, envigorating experience, that will give them fulfillment and a pride of accomplishment
- provide a social situation where the elderly may meet other elderly with similar adjustment problems
- teach basic techniques of an art discipline
- provide activities that use fine motor skills
- create community awareness of the talents of their elderly
- open communication among the elderly, middle-aged community participants and local school children
- encourage local artists to continue the arts/elderly program
- attract local financial support of future programs

The Theater

The Greensboro Health Care Center in North Carolina operates the Senior Theatre consortium, which is made up of local organizations. Nursing home residents participate in theater productions and seminars on aging.

When planning, the consortium committee addressed the following areas, which are mentioned in the program's literature:

(1) Audience—Church clubs and civic organizations, volunteers, patients of Greensboro Health Care Center, retirement communities, Greensboro Urban Ministries, Association for the Advancement of Retired Persons, Department of Social Services, and the general public.

(2) Project participants—A total of 1,000 participants (Health Care Center—175, Parks and Recreation—350, United Services for Older Adults—175, Community Theater of Greensboro—300)—enough participants for seven daytime performances and three nighttime performances for the general public for a total of ten seminars.

(3) Modes of transportation for the project—The Parks and Recreation Department of the City of Greensboro has three buses (capacity per bus: 32) that can be used during daytime hours. Other transportation resources are available including church buses.

(4) Budget

a. Staff time:

Greensboro Health Care Center (2 staff × 80 hrs. @ $8)	$1,280
United Services for Older Adults (100 hrs. @ $8/hr)	800
Parks and Recreation (100 hrs. @ $8/hr)	800
Moderators (30 moderators @ $25/seminar)	750
Subtotal	$3,630

b. Promotion, printing and videotaping:

Greensboro Health Care Center (videotaping)	$1,500
Typesetting and programs (4,000 copies)	955
Parks and Recreation, USOA (flyers)	450
All groups combined (postage)	177
Subtotal	$3,082

c. Rehearsal and production assistance:

Community Theatre of Greensboro	$1,250

d. Transportation and related costs:

Parks and Recreation (buses, drivers and mileage)	774
Total	$8,736

e. In addition to the cash contributions and in-kind donations of Consortium members, the following expenses will be incurred:

Artistic Director	$1,000
Production Stage Manager	250
Facility Rental	500
Scripts	105
Royalties	365
Miscellaneous	35
	$2,255

Karol Verson was Artistic Director for Acting Up. This group has thirteen members sixty-five and older. Verson stated that "there are three stages to what we do. One is storytelling and memory sharing. That's important, because that's where the material comes from. Second is theater games and improvisations. The third stage is performance. A lot of groups don't want to go to performance; they just want to have a good time and have fun. And that's fine; you can do the process without having to go out and perform."

The group has expressed an interest in developing a senior soap opera for television. Verson said that she has talked to a producer about a show for local cable TV. For further information, contact Ms. Verson at College of DuPage, Illinois.

Recordings for Recovery

This group supplies without charge music of therapeutic value, to people suffering from physical, mental or emotional problems. It was started by Ralph Hoy, a musician and conductor. The service includes identifying problems, gathering data, and producing audiotapes of musical selections. In twenty-five countries, more than 500,000 persons—children, adolescents, geriatric, retarded, and chronic patients—have benefited from this service.

The Pennsylvania State University has now joined with this service to increase recovery opportunities for individuals in general, children's and veterans' hospitals, prisons, nursing homes, and individuals confined to their homes. A music library of more than 22,000 selections includes classical music, band music, childrens' programs, and religious music. Professionals in medicine, human services, music, music therapy, special education, nursing, psychology, and therapeutic recreation, and 250 volunteers enable the organization to increase its activities. Donations and private foundation monies provide funding.

This service is free of charge. Programs are loaned for limited periods of time. Individuals can keep tapes permanently if they provide high quality blank tapes to be programmed for others. On page 89 is an excerpt from the Penn State application form.

Literature

Sharon Reilly-Marosy, a Counselor for the East Brunswick, N.J. Department of Recreation and Parks, furnished information about

APPLICATION FORM:

_____ _____ _____
Name   Name of organization   Location and telephone number

_____ _____
Group or type of individuals   Specific physical and mental condition

_____ _____
Personnel in charge   Staff   Types of music preferred

_____ _____ _____ _____ _____
Talent (if any) Equipment Ages of patients Religion Mobility

For special individuals, list names, hobbies and background _____

_____

Patient Attitudes

_____ Depressed   _____ Despondent   _____ Hyperactive

Type of Program Preferred

_____ Classical   _____ Adults   _____ Folk music

_____ Length of program _____ Light classical _____ Piano

_____ Religious music   _____ Story songs   _____ Organ

_____ Instrumental   _____ Children

   Please attach a letter stating any special information which will aid in selection of material. Are you interested in building a permanent library for use by your group?

_____
Signature   Date

Mail to: New Kensington Campus—Continuing Education
The Pennsylvania State University
3550 Seventh Street Road
New Kensington, PA 15068

"Poetry by the Pond," a group which meets once a week by a pond to read and discuss poetry. There are both intellectual and psychosocial dimensions to this group. She observed,

> Programs such as "Poetry by the Pond" help the elderly on several levels. My goal is to offer an atmosphere of warmth and acceptance which will encourage sharing. Many of the elderly with whom I work live alone. This group offers an intellectually stimulating experience as well as the warmth of human interaction. The good feelings which ensue because someone listens and responds to thoughts and feelings encourages a sense of self-esteem, self-worth and companionship. As people live longer and lose family and friend support systems, help is needed to establish new support systems. Starting all over again at age seventy-five can be a very difficult task. "Poetry by the Pond" is a way to open the door for new companions without the embarrassment or anxiety often accompanied by meeting new people.

The home study course Yarns of Yesteryear is an outgrowth of a contest which the University of Wisconsin has sponsored. Many of the participants found writing their reminiscences for the contest so satisfying that they wanted help in continuing this worthwhile leisure time activity. Some have gone on to write complete autobiographies for their families and many have had their stories published.

The course content is centered around these basic questions:

- What shall I write?
- How shall I write it?
- How can I improve what I have written?
- How do I research the history of my own backyard?
- Can I use personal reminiscences in writing articles, essays, drama, fiction and children's stories?
- Is there a market for my memories?

Gen Lewis, director of this project, stated that:

> We have had comments from several families, that writing reminiscences gave their older members a new and challenging way to fill their leisure time and in one case, helped a woman overcome her depression at having to go into a nursing home. One of the reasons for the good effects, I believe, is that family members take a real interest in the project. They are eager to get down in print all that information about their parents' early life, as a matter of family history.
>
> We have had similar comments about the Yarns of Yesteryear Contest which the University has been sponsoring for the past twelve years. The annual contest gives older people a reason to put down in writing some of their reminiscences, and their families are intrigued and interested

. . . and sometimes surprised. One contestant told us that her daughter, after reading her contest entry, said to her, "Why didn't you tell us about that?" Her response was, "Because you never asked!"

Family Participation

In a nursing home I am acquainted with, families participate in parties at holiday times. Residents wear nice dress and eagerly wait for party time. Families bring in special food and treats. Staff decorate the dining room and dress up. Often families and staff bring in their children. There are comedy skits. A hired band plays songs that residents remember from their youth.

I have noted that sing-alongs quiet and relax even confused residents of a nursing home. One of my favorite residents used to sing classic Italian songs. I remembered hearing my Dad singing the same songs, and so I would join her in a duet in Italian. At other times, she became quite confused and people told me it was lucky my Italian was limited, so I did not understand that I was being told off. However, when she heard music or sang she was happy and relaxed.

Another good thing families can do is volunteer their skills. Residents enjoy participating in sculpture classes or crafts. Their work can be exhibited at the parties. Singing in a choir is an activity enjoyed by residents. On occasion, families whose elderly relative dies in the home "adopt" another resident, whose family does not visit. They bring small gifts, pictures and treats.

Residents who have always enjoyed reading really miss it when their vision becomes impaired. Talking books are a possible solution to this problem. Another approach is to combine socialization and literature appreciation by having a family volunteer assist interested residents (ambulatory or in wheelchairs) to form a book discussion group or current affairs group. Even if the nursing home is fortunate to employ staff in therapeutic recreation, they can expand their offerings if they have assistance from volunteer help.

Suggestion

1 Look for creative activities which all the adults in your family would have the opportunity to participate in, if they expressed an interest in doing so.

legal and ethical concerns

Family members should become aware of the most common legal problems that their elderly relatives face. Wayne Moore, of the Legal Counsel for the Elderly in Washington, D.C., observed that the most frequently asked questions by callers concerned issues of guardianship, probate, wills, and protective services. Other areas of frequency included issues on housing, financial problems, consumer practices, and torts (e.g., automobile, discrimination, criminal, small business, neighbor disputes, employment, social services). A portion of the callers also had questions regarding Medicare/Medicaid, taxes, food stamps and other public benefits.

Moore described a legal advice service as follows:

> The Legal Hotline currently operates in Allegheny County, Pennsylvania, as a pilot project of Legal Counsel for the Elderly and sponsored by the American Association for Retired Persons. The service provides free legal advice by telephone to residents of the county age sixty and older. The callers describe their problems to attorneys who are experienced in the matters of elderly law. If it is determined that action should be taken in the interest of the caller, the attorney will refer him/her to one of several selected attorneys who charge negotiated low rates.
>
> The primary goal of the Hotline is to offer older persons the information they need to determine if they have a legal problem. Once informed, they can better choose whether to resolve their problem independently or with additional help from referral attorneys. In this way, the Hotline promotes independence among the elderly community.
>
> The objective of the project is twofold:
>
> (1) To provide a telephone service which is solely dedicated to resolv-

ing the majority of older people's legal problems and questions at no charge

(2) To financially support this service by providing other services for a low fee and by referring callers whose legal problems can't be solved on the phone to lawyers who are willing to reduce their fees and help financially support the project in return for the high volume of business

None of the attorneys staffing the Hotline are allowed to accept referrals. All their case notes which document the advice given are reviewed by two supervisors for accuracy and thoroughness. The attorneys meet biweekly to receive feedback from the supervisors and to share information on commonly occurring client legal problems. Most information programs do not provide legal information; and few, if any, provide advice.

Legal information is information that is generally applicable to people in the same circumstances. For example, the proposition that "people who are terminated from SSA benefits are entitled to a hearing to review the decision" is legal information, which can be provided by non-lawyers. Legal advice involves applying legal information to a person's specific situation and recommending actions that should be taken. For example, "You should request a SSA hearing" is legal advice. Only lawyers licensed to practice in a state are allowed to give legal advice. Only lawyers licensed to practice in a state are allowed to give legal advice in that state.

The major source of funding comes from attorneys who pay the project 16.6 percent of their fees in exchange for referrals. Callers are charged a $15 referral fee, which entitles the caller to a free half hour consultation with an attorney. Wills are drafted by Hotline attorneys for $45. A brief service, such as writing a letter or making a phone call to a third person, costs $20.

An Elderly Legal Services Program

Marie Salter made available information about the Elderly Legal Services program of the Southwest Georgia Area Agency on Aging (SOWEGA). The area of Southwest Georgia consists of fourteen rural counties. Of 33,901 people over sixty-five in this area, 10,164 were below the poverty level, making them prime targets for swindles and deals by the unscrupulous.

Salter reviewed the program's operation:

A paralegal makes the initial contact with a client, to assess his needs. Clients are referred to an appropriate agency or a volunteer lawyer, if this is considered to be advisable. The initial consultation is free.

Monthly visits are scheduled by the paralegal to all of the senior centers, and periodic contact is made with the nursing homes in the area. Volunteer attorneys visit the senior centers to speak on such topics as wills, Social Security, and remarriage and older adults. The paralegal conducts programs for senior centers on subjects ranging from testifying in court to funeral planning.

When private attorneys are motivated, organized, and encouraged, they willingly volunteer their time to represent the elderly. In addition to the self-satisfaction received in helping resolve problems encountered by the elderly, the volunteer attorneys broaden their experience and receive recognition from the community for the services they provide.

Estate Planning Checklist

The Bureau of Maine's Elderly developed the following estate planning checklist for families.

ESTATE PLANNING CHECKLIST

I. Family Information
    A. PERSONAL: Client   Spouse
        1. Name
        2. Home Address
        3. Home Phone
        4. Employer & Business Address
        5. Birth Date
        6. Status of Health
        7. Place of Birth
           (citizenship)
        8. Social Security Number
        9. Date & Place of Marriage
        10. Prior Marriages
    B. YOUR CHILDREN: (Indicate if child of prior marriage)
        Name and Address   Birth Date
    C. PARTICULARS REGARDING YOUR GRANDCHILDREN
        Their Parents   Names of Grandchildren   Birth Date
    D. OTHER BENEFICIARIES—names, addresses, and relationships

II. Summary of Assets and Liabilities
    A. ASSETS   Husband   Wife   Joint
        1. Cash
        2. Bank Accounts
        3. Bonds
        4. Listed Stocks

     5. Business Interest
     6. Real Estate
     7. Insurance
     8. Employment Benefits
     9. Personal Effects (clothing, furnishings)
    10. Cars
    11. Trust Interests
    12. Miscellaneous (describe)

B. LIABILITIES
     1. Real Estate Mortgages
     2. Notes to Banks, etc.
     3. Loans on Insurance Policies
     4. Tax Liabilities
     5. Other Obligations (describe)

III. Plan for Disposition

A. Lifetime Objectives:

B. Provision for Spouse at Death:
Is There a Need for Professional Management?

C. Provision for Children at Death:
Is There a Need for Professional Management?

D. Provisions for Other Beneficiaries:

E. Gifts to Charities:

IV. Advisors & Important Documents

A. ADVISORS: Name   Address   Telephone
     1. Attorney
     2. Clergyman
     3. Physician
     4. Life Insurance Adv.
     5. Accountant
     6. Bank Officer
     7. Other Advisor (Identify)
     8. Have you ever given someone Power of Attorney?
     9. Do you have a Conservator?
    10. Do you have a Guardian?
    11. Who will be Personal Representative
       (Executor of your will)
    12. Who will be Trustee for any Trust?

B. DOCUMENTS: Date   Location
     1. Will
     2. Power of Attorney
     3. Trust
     4. Income Tax Return
     5. Deeds

    6. Insurance Policies
    7. Divorce/Separation Papers
    8. Antenuptial Agreement
    9. Other Documents (describe)
C. Do you have a safety deposit box?   Keys:
   Owner(s):   Location:

Consumer Fraud

Elderly people are at a disadvantage in making home repairs, because they can't climb on a roof to check if it really needs repairs. Door-to-door salesmen or mail-order sellers may persuade people to sign a contract with spaces not filled in. Under certain conditions, a buyer has three days to change his mind about a door-to-door purchase. However, people are sometimes embarrassed to admit that they were "stupid" enough to be conned.

For more information, read the Federal Trade Commission's booklet *How to Write a Wrong*. This gives advice on how to issue a complaint. It is available from the Office of Consumer and Business Education, Bureau of Consumer Protection, Washington, DC 20580. For a free booklet that provides a listing of government agencies and private organizations that can help resolve complaints, ask for the *Consumer's Resource Handbook*, Dept. 579L, Pueblo, Colorado, 81009.

Family Friends

Healthy elderly volunteers can be consumer advocates for the frail elderly and for people of all ages. An example of this is the Family Friends Program, directed by Meridith Miller, of the National Council on Aging. This program pairs older volunteers with families with chronically ill or disabled children. While some families are able to handle the physical, emotional and financial problems in this situation, for other families the stress can be too much. Such families experience higher rates of divorce and child abuse.

The role of the Family Friends generally could be described as grandparenting. They assist children and families in five areas:

- social and emotional support, offering friendship, guidance, and companionship
- recreational and cultural activities including arts, crafts, athletics, and outings

- supplemental educational activities building on the child's developmental stimulation programs or school assignments
- advocacy, such as helping the family learn about and obtain services available in the community, or assisting in working with professionals and institutions
- self-help and personal care skills, such as helping the child feed, wash, or dress independently

Family Friends also assist parents by serving as positive role models, teaching behavior management techniques, and providing respite from unusual burdens of parenting a disabled or chronically ill child.

Meridith Miller, Program Director, informed me that this project increased the volunteers' self-esteem. Women who were lonely, depressed or isolated gained a whole new outlook on life through the Family Friends Project. How does a Family Friend volunteer help a family in trouble? The following case study was provided from the Family Friends Project.

Mrs. L. J., a Family Friend, is a sixty-four-year-old black woman who grew up in a poor, rural environment in southern Maryland. As the oldest of three children, she soon developed a sense of responsibility. After graduating from high school with an excellent grade point average, she was unable to attend college because of financial limitations. She has worked in a variety of settings as a nursing assistant, from a nursing home to a state hospital for the mentally retarded.

Mrs. L. J. had seven children. She was responsible for the total support of her children, as her husband, from whom she separated, was never employed. She worked at two jobs while her children were growing up. She was never on welfare and her children are now employed, responsible citizens. Mrs. L. J. takes special pride in one of her sons who is classified as mentally retarded, but who lives independently. She has consistently stood up for this son's rights and waged many battles with various educational and social agencies in order to ensure that he was provided with the best possible services.

To supplement an income of less than $5,000, Mrs. L. J. spends five nights a week as a companion to an elderly woman. Mrs. L. J. was on a waiting list for the local Foster Grandparent program when she was contacted by the Family Friends Program. This program has given her extra income while allowing her to use the advocacy skills developed over the years. She is matched with an inner city family, the T.'s, headed by a mildly mentally retarded woman who has three children, ages thirteen, twelve, and ten. All of the children are mildly retarded and, in addition, the twelve-year-old has a seizure condition.

Mrs. L. J. has had a significant impact on the T. family. She has helped Mrs. T. apply for Supplemental Security Income for the children. This has resulted in a substantial increase in income for the family. Mrs. L. J. has assisted Mrs. T. in obtaining winter clothing for the children and food from various community groups. She has taught Mrs. T. how to budget her limited income and how to shop for groceries. She has developed strong ties with the three T. children and is available to them for grandmotherly support and attention as well as assistance with their homework. She has been to the children's schools to speak with their teachers and has encouraged Mrs. T. to participate more actively in the children's school activities.

One of the major areas in which Mrs. L. J. has made a difference for the T.'s is in housing. They live in a substandard home in need of many repairs, which the landlord refused to do. After the kitchen ceiling collapsed and water covered the floor, Mrs. L. J. brought Mrs. T. to the neighborhood community legal services office. Mrs. T. is now paying her rent into a court-ordered escrow account until all necessary repairs are made. Plans have been made to sue the landlord for damages.

Mrs. L. J. has been able to maintain her objectivity with the T.'s and is consistent in her efforts to encourage Mrs. T.'s independence. She has been very effective in bolstering Mrs. T.'s confidence and in encouraging Mrs. T. to stand up for herself in spite of her limitations. This match is an excellent example of the mutual benefits that can be reaped from an intergenerational program and the resources offered by nonprofessionals who have a wealth of valuable life experience. Mrs. L. J. feels needed by this family. She has been able to use her knowledge of community resources to help the T.s, which at the same time has bolstered her own self-esteem. Her involvement with the T.s has resulted in her being offered a position on the community advisory board of the neighborhood legal services office. As Mrs. L. J. stated, "I may bring them more business than they want."

The Friend/Advocate

Sharon Mitchell, Program Supervisor, described the Community Health Law Project's Friend/Advocate Program, in East Orange, New Jersey:

> The main thrust of the Friend/Advocate Program is to promote independence and offset institutionalization through the advocacy efforts and assistance of trained volunteers. Not only do volunteers attempt to mobilize existing resources to benefit their clients, but in some cases, they may initiate or develop resources where no other exists.

Volunteers and clients develop a trusting relationship which enhances the advocacy and assistance that can be provided. In many cases, volunteers are able to accomplish more than social service providers as a result of such a relationship with their clients. Additionally, many state and social service agencies have been very receptive toward volunteers, because they are acting as a community member concerned for the welfare of another.

The Friend/Advocate Program is funded by the Essex County Division on Aging. It was established to address the needs of the frail and vulnerable elderly living independently in Essex County. Volunteers receive training in advocacy techniques; physical, social, and emotional needs of the elderly; legal resources; problem-solving techniques; dealing with emergency situations.

Volunteers are linked with an elderly client with whom they contact to check on well-being, explore and obtain available services in the community, assist with decision-making, budgeting, paying bills, and arranging medical care and transportation. Advocacy and friendship are two important components by which the Friend/Advocate can ease the loneliness and isolation of their elderly client and provide an important link with the community and the services offered by the community. The volunteers increase social contacts, as well as increasing utilization and knowledge of resources for the older person.

The following cases are taken from the Friend/Advocate files.

1. Mrs. R., eighty-four years old, had been living alone for close to twenty years. Because of a severe visual impairment, a close friend had been helping Mrs. R. with her shopping, banking, mail reading, and bill paying. When this friend moved to Florida last year, Mrs. R. experienced a terrible loss. Left with no one to assist her, Mrs. R. was stopping people in the hallway of her apartment building, as well as on the street, to ask for assistance. Predictably, many of the passers-by took advantage of the opportunity and Mrs. R. was robbed several times. Mrs. R. was introduced to a volunteer from the program, who has been able to assist her with opening a checking account and getting direct deposit of her Social Security check, so banking and bill paying would be easier. Additionally, the volunteer was able to speed up Mrs. R.'s application for senior housing because of her unsafe living conditions and rough neighborhood. The volunteer visits weekly to assist with shopping, banking, mail reading, and bill paying. She is in the process of obtaining a chore service for Mrs. R. to assist with household tasks.

2. Mrs. B., eighty-six years old, has lived in her apartment for fifty years. Her husband died in 1980, and her son died in 1983, leaving Mrs. B. alone to take care of herself and her apartment. Mrs. B.'s monthly income consisted of $300 per month and she was forced to live on a savings account of $1000.

The volunteer recognized that her client might be eligible for SSI and Food Stamps, so she filed applications. While sorting through Mrs. B.'s papers, the volunteer came across a $20,000 life insurance policy for Mrs. B.'s dead son. Mrs. B. received a check for this amount from the company.

The volunteer informed the Social Security and Food Stamp offices to inform them of this increase in income. Mrs. B. then opened a bank account. The volunteer continues to assist Mrs. B. with her banking and bill paying.

3. Mrs. M., an eighty-four-year-old widow, was accustomed to the bank, which held a trust account for her, paying her bills on a regular basis. When the bank contacted Mrs. M. to inform her that her resources could no longer cover the expense of her live-in aide and that she should consider a nursing home, Mrs. M. adamantly refused. The bank then brought in two doctors to attest to her competency. Then the bank petitioned the court for guardianship and a guardian was appointed.

Mr. H., the guardian, is an attorney with very little knowledge of the social service system. He requested assistance to help Mrs. M. remain in her home. The plan we developed and assisted Mr. H. with coordinating included:

- personal care (bathing, meals)
- household assistance (housekeeping, home repairs, shopping)
- transportation
- financial assistance (tax deductions, energy assistance, pharmaceutical assistance and bill paying assistance)

Ethics and the Volunteer Guardian

In all of the community projects described in this chapter, there is a strong commitment to acting according to ethical principles in interaction with the elderly person. A strong focus of these programs is on maintaining independence and showing respect for the wishes of the elderly person. Sometimes it is very difficult for a relative to facilitate an elderly person living at home with assistance, when the relative perceives that the person would be safer and better cared for in a nursing home. The situation becomes even more complex when the relative is asked to become the guardian of an elderly person who has diminished mental competency. This is especially the case when the elderly person has episodes of confusion, but is alert for part of the time and knows he is "losing his mind."

Ms. Savannah Sledge, Coordinator, provided the following information about the Volunteer Guardian program of the Family Service of Milwaukee:

In 1976 the Department of Social Services formed an Adult Protective Services Unit, to investigate claims of elder abuse and related incidents.

The Protective Service Management Team (PSMT) prepares for incompetency proceedings in court and assigns proposed guardians to persons in need of protection. To place a person in protected placement, a nursing home must have sixteen beds or more.

In previous years, half the people had family members as guardians. Since the 1976 requirement that nursing homes and institutions arrange evaluations for all potentially incompetent residents, 2,500 residents without family were referred to PSMT as needing a Volunteer Guardian.

In 1979, the Department of Social Services contracted with Family Service for establishing a Volunteer Guardian program. As of December, 1985, 419 screened volunteers were referred for training to PSMT. Over 200 guardians have more than one resident; the maximum is five residents per guardian. One-third of the volunteers are employees or former employees of nursing homes or county institutions. The guardian is required to visit the resident once a month to observe care and interaction between the staff and the resident, and if there are concerns to voice them with the appropriate staff person. The Guardian interacts with the staff, physicians, government and private agencies in an attempt to bring about a satisfactory solution for all involved parties.

Here are examples of situations that have taken place between Volunteer Guardians and residents:

An elderly Volunteer Guardian sat at a nursing home bedside chatting about her youth and children. The Guardian wondered if the old lady who stared lifelessly up at her, knew, or even cared whether she visited or not. But one day, perhaps out of her own frustrations, the volunteer took the old lady's hand and said, "I am only going to visit one day a month from now on." The old lady weakly squeezed the Guardian's hand and a tear slipped silently down her cheek. The Guardian continued her weekly visits, knowing that her visits did make a difference.

A Guardian entered the nursing home to meet his resident for the first time. His resident was a cantankerous eighty-two-year-old wheelchair-bound gentleman. He was a double amputee who swore at the aides, and used all kinds of abusive language. Although very verbal, the gentleman was quite confused and angry. The Guardian sat down and listened quietly to the stream of language until the resident became calm. After one and a half years of this relationship, the resident is less hostile. He has learned to play chess and tells the Guardian's son stories of the Great War. The Guardian knew that he had made a difference.

The Guardian checked the resident's account. The resident was entitled to $45 of his $363/month Social Security payments for his personal use. A supplement for his medical care was paid to the home. The Guardian asked the administrator why the resident was being charged for shoes and socks. The administrator told the Guardian that the nursing home purchased them for residents with no family. The Guardian then asked the administrator, 'Are you aware that the resident is a double amputee?'"

The one-to-one relationship between resident and Guardian is very unique. Each Guardian brings strong personal attributes which serve to enhance and strengthen that relationship. A nursing home can be a lonely and frightening experience, especially when residents are unable to understand what is happening to them.

The Volunteer Guardian Association provides an avenue for Guardians to share their concerns and solutions for those concerns. In-service training is provided once monthly. Outside speakers come from funeral homes, nursing homes, government agencies, Social Security, Title XIX and include legal counselors, PSMT and other lay people.

Suggestions

1 Appreciate the legal and ethical concerns involved in aging.
2 <u>Handicaps</u>: Job Accommodation Network (800)526-7234, (800) 526-4698 in West Virginia. If needed, check this resource which offers ideas for accommodating handicapped persons in the workplace. Provides information on the availability of accommodation aids and procedures.

shelter

Having the ability to choose where one lives is a concept many Americans take for granted. However, for many older people that choice is not available. Senior citizens frequently find themselves in housing unsuitable for their physical, financial or emotional needs. Often, some accurate and timely information can solve the problem before it becomes critical. CHOICE, a housing counseling program administered by the Colorado Association of Aging, is intended to fill this need. The following is taken from literature describing the organization provided by Anoel Rinaldi, Information Specialist.

CHOICE was developed to counsel older people on a one-to-one basis, as to the most appropriate housing for their health, income, and social and psychological needs. The counseling, ninety-eight percent of which takes place in the client's home, is done by a social worker with Master's training and experience in working with the elderly and their families. This housing specialist is knowledgeable about those agencies and services which help people remain in their own homes, and about the availability of units in senior buildings, rooms in personal care homes, nursing homes, subsidized housing, adult day care centers, and home health agencies.

The person's current living space may be made adequate with the help of social services or community volunteers, such as homemaker services to do shopping and cleaning, home health service for personal or nursing care, Meals on Wheels to provide ready-to-eat food, transportation and private duty nursing. Even after the person has found a suitable home, the counselor continues to monitor the situation.

Gail Zink, CHOICE Counselor, noted, "Each person has different needs as they grow older. However, few people give up the desire to be independent. Our job is to keep that spark of independence alive." CHOICE provides as much information to families of senior citizens as they do to the senior citizens themselves. Many families are not aware of the alternatives available in housing for the elderly. The counselors encourage input from the family.

"A third aspect of CHOICE is the community education program. Far too many people wait for a crisis before they begin looking for alternative housing. The objective of the community education program is to present alternatives when the specter of panic isn't sitting on one's shoulder. Presentations on Housing Options for Seniors are given to community groups, such as groups for the elderly, service organizations, church groups, professional organizations, and as in-service workshops to hospital staffs. In addition, CHOICE offers technical assistance to local developers of housing for the elderly."

A critical element in providing shelter for the elderly is enlisting community support. In my own state of Illinois, there is a small village, Murdock, with 151 people—twenty percent of whom are elderly. A Murdock housewife, Marjorie Shearer, recognized the problem that there was no ground-level building in which persons with limited mobility could meet and interact socially.

A member of Mrs. Shearer's family donated land. She contacted a local contractor and mobilized a team of enthusiastic volunteers to build the Little Hall on the Prairie. This hall is the only ground floor meeting place available within a 20-mile radius.

The hall is a community center for blood pressure screening, recreation, bingo, education about nutrition, etc., a kitchen band—the Sunshine Guys and Gals. Little Hall offers innovative programming and service, community involvement, volunteerism, cost effectiveness and enhancement of the quality of life of its citizens.

Marion Dolan, R.N., of Heritage Home Health provided information about People Match, a home-sharing program which helps the elderly by "alleviating the loneliness and isolation which often accompanies living alone." In addition, it helps to match wealth and health with mutual benefits. People Match can help:

- a single adult who needs another person to help meet financial obligations
- a couple who needs assistance because of poor health or lack of wealth
- a student who needs a home
- a professional who wants a place to live

- to be a choice and an alternative to institutional placement
- to be an opportunity to live in the community you prefer
- to establish a home-like setting
- to achieve the power to live the way you choose

"How does the process work? Home visits + written assessment + video screening + computer search + pre-match meeting = People Match. By sharing expenses the average person is able to increase his income by $2,000 to $6,000 a year." The following is the assessment tool used by People Match.

Housing Preference:
☐SINGLE HOUSE   ☐APARTMENTS   ☐SHARED OR GROUP HOME

Three possessions I have that I couldn't live without:

Recreational Interests:

Organizational Affiliations:

Is there any health symptoms you would not be able to tolerate?
☐COUGH   ☐COLOSTOMY   ☐AMPUTATION   ☐DEAFNESS   ☐BLINDNESS
☐OTHER

Chores or services that need to be performed:

What support services do you have in your area?
☐HOME HEALTH AGENCY   ☐MEALS ON WHEELS   ☐COMMUNITY SERVICES
☐OTHER

What future plans do you have:

What part of New Hampshire do you wish to relocate to?

Do you want to stay in your present location?

Would you prefer paying for a companion?
☐YES   ☐NO   ☐PART-TIME   ☐FULL-TIME

Give three towns or cities you would consider:

What type of location is preferable?
☐CITY   ☐RURAL   ☐NEAR WATER   ☐NEAR SHOPPING   ☐NEAR MOUNTAINS

Need Companion: ☐MALE   ☐FEMALE

Bed Time: ☐9-11 P.M.   ☐11-2 A.M.   ☐AFTER 2 A.M.

Rising Hour:

Meals: ☐2 A DAY   ☐3 A DAY   ☐MORE THAN 3 A DAY

Special Dietary Needs:

Do you cook?   ☐YES   ☐NO

Three foods you like:

Three foods you dislike:

Personal Habits:

	Yes	No
STAIRS	☐	☐
READING	☐	☐
SMOKING	☐	☐
ALCOHOL	☐	☐
T.V.	☐	☐
LOUD MUSIC	☐	☐
FRIED FOODS	☐	☐
BATH TUB	☐	☐
SHOWER	☐	☐
DOG	☐	☐
CAT	☐	☐
TRAVEL	☐	☐
AUTOMOBILE	☐	☐
DINING OUT	☐	☐
CARDS, GAMES, PUZZLES	☐	☐
VISITORS	☐	☐
LONG PHONE CONVERSATIONS	☐	☐

Financial Expectations of the Other Party:

This assessment also includes basic information questions about name, address, age, marital status, religion, and relatives and children.

Homesharing

Another example of shared housing is Homesharing. Kevin Wilcoxon, network coordinator at Penn Valley Community College, Missouri, presented the following data about Homesharing:

The professional staff screens and refers both householders and home-seekers, who then decide upon their specific arrangements. Home-sharing requires interviews and reference checks. The responsibilities of each person are written in an agreement and signed by both parties.
Homesharing typically helps:

- the elderly who seek companionship, need help with rising utility costs or help in managing the upkeep of their homes
- anyone in transition: divorce, death of spouse, career change, new in town, unable to afford traditional housing
- students seeking low-cost housing and willing to provide assistance with household chores

Homesharing cannot serve those in need of intensive or 24-hour care. Most Homesharing matches fall into one of the following categories:

(1) The sharer pays the homeowner an amount of money.

(2) The sharer does not pay any money, but performs specified tasks in exchange for room and board.

(3) The sharer pays a reduced amount of money in exchange for certain tasks.

(4) The sharer receives room and board in exchange for tasks, and is also paid a specified amount by the homeowner.

After registering, participants are interviewed and references checked. The staff suggests possible matches. Identities remain confidential, until permission to make introductions is given. If they decide to share, an agreement is negotiated so that everyone clearly understands what is expected of the sharing arrangement. Staff members are available for consultation, and participants are encouraged to keep in touch. The more flexible the participants can be, the sooner an appropriate match can be made.

The following chart is a profile of persons involved in the Homesharing program.

Homesharing Project Service Statistics

Intakes Completed	1,616	
Householders 53%	Homeseekers 47%	
Information & Referrals	390	
Interviews Completed	601	
Householders 39%	Homeseekers 61%	
Match Referrals	870	
Matches Completed	162	
Persons Involved	413	
Disability 15%	Minority 8%	Low & Moderate Income 86%
Terminations	120	
Acceptable/		
"Natural" 77%	Unsatisfactory 23% (Incompatibility, Lack of Privacy, Failure to Abide by Contract)	
Active Matches 98	Persons Involved 248	
Householder Characteristics:		
Most Common Age 70s	Female 69%	Widowed/ Divorced 71%

Employed at least 3/4 time   44%   Retired   49%
Homeseeker Characteristics:
Most Common Age   20s   Male   47%   Never Married   71%
Employed   43%   Student   45%

Mary G., age fifty-eight, was set out on the street by her landlord, with furniture piled on the apartment house lawn. When ex-husband stopped alimony payments, Mary was unprepared to support herself, since she has a back injury and no history of employment. Mary stayed in a local shelter that night, and went to the Salvation Army Senior Center for help in applying for assistance and legal aid. The Salvation Army and Homesharing provided transportation for Mary to visit potential sharers.

Within two weeks, Mary entered into a sharing arrangement with seventy-seven-year-old R. B., who has a heart condition requiring regular medication and other treatment. Mary sees that R. B. maintains her medication schedule, prepares meals and helps with housekeeping in exchange for room and board. Mary's ex-husband eventually restarted alimony payments, at which time Mary began helping with utility bills. Mary has been sharing about eight months now.

According to Wilcoxon, there has been an increase in the number of inquirers with needs inappropriate to Homesharing: those in need of assistance but without necessary space; persons needing emergency housing; the emotionally ill; single parents with two or more children; and elderly persons in need of 24-hour care.

Nursing Home Projects

Larry Blitz is administrator of Mission Skilled Nursing Facility in Santa Clara, California. He perceives that lack of communication is the source of problems in the nursing home field. Blitz noted, "Myths and public misunderstanding about long-term care make effective communication with the public absolutely essential."

The Santa Clara Chapter of the California Association of Health Facilities has set up a 24-hour nursing home hot-line. Consumers can call providers of goods and services to sort out problems, become better informed and, sometimes, seek needed psychological support.

Seven Santa Clara professionals—administrators, nurses, etc.— answer questions from consumers referred to them by volunteer operators. These professionals need a broad knowledge of the complex facets of long-term care and the ability to communicate their knowledge.

Since referrals are made on a rotating basis, each professional must be prepared to answer questions that might not be about his or her direct responsibility in the facility. These people meet once a week to review calls and responses. The Santa Clara group provided the following information:

Establishing a Hot-Line—A separate phone with its own line and number should be in a quiet setting—never in a skilled nursing facility to protect confidentiality. The volunteers should have an established procedure:

(1) Credibility is crucial. The volunteer must exude warmth and understanding.

(2) A log kept next to the telephone should be used to write down the date, time, and the nature of each call, as well as the name of the person to whom the call is referred.

(3) Volunteers should not communicate with the caller beyond getting the caller's phone number. They should not discuss the complaint or offer answers.

Proper call handling—The anonymity of the caller must be respected. All callers must be told that the Hot-Line is sponsored by a non-profit trade association and has no connection with government or consumer advocacy group. Callers must be treated with courtesy. Many calls will be repeat questions, but professionals must listen patiently and with interest, as if they had never been asked the question before. Encourage callers to talk freely. At no time should the caller be cut off with a "yes, but" or any similar reaction. Don't be defensive!

Typical calls—Patient care problems or life-threatening situations must be referred to an outside agency, to protect the elderly person involved and to protect the personnel staffing the Hot-Line. Members of the Hot-Line must avoid recommending or rating facilities when asked about placement of a relative. Offer to send them a copy of the American Health Care Association's *Thinking About a Nursing Home.* Callers seeking information about how to pay for care should be given the name of the local Medicaid or Medicare office. While it is appropriate to discuss such programs in principle, only the outside agency is qualified to determine eligibility. Callers with complaints should be strongly urged to discuss the problem with the facility administrator or director of nursing.

Following up—If the caller asks the professional to intervene with a facility, a follow-up call must be made, to inform the caller of action and results. Summaries of calls should be open to public inspection as a way to demonstrate to the community that professionals involved in daily, hands-on care delivery can resolve complaints and disseminate information.

Mr. Blitz believes that the California Hot-Line has been successful because it has been perceived by the public as a patient-oriented community service, and by association members as a way that providers can help and advise fellow providers when necessary. For further information, contact Mr. Blitz at (408)248-3736.

Judy Lupien is director of Volunteer Services at the Home for the Elderly, Glencliff, N.H., which is located in a very rural area, twenty miles from the nearest large town and available services. The state-owned facility is home to 132 elderly residents with a history of long-term institutionalization at the state hospital. Ms. Lupien stated that:

> The philosophy of the facility is to treat residents with dignity and respect. The treatment goal is to provide the least restrictive environment possible while keeping residents physically and mentally active, thereby increasing their independence and self-worth.
>
> Project Mini-Bus and Varied Trips have done a great deal to promote independence for our residents. Examples of trips are as follows:

(1) Medical—With the automatic lift, the mini-bus is easily accessible for wheelchairs. The bus is used to take residents in wheelchairs to doctor's appointments. Also we have gone to visit a resident in the hospital.

(2) Nutritional—Our residents love to eat in a variety of settings—picinics, MacDonald's, coffee shops, and for supper to the elegant and formal atmosphere of the Mount Washington Hotel.

(3) Shopping—These trips are usually in conjunction with a luncheon trip. Residents shop for clothing, cosmetics, cards and gifts, groceries (fruit, candy), yarn, and craft supplies.

(4) Educational—Our trips take us to maple sugar operations, libraries, museums, and many scenic attractions. Each year we write for a free pass to the state parks.

(5) Social and Recreational—Bowling, miniature golf, parades, plays, concerts, fairs, shows, field days, church services, hay rides, and parties. For those who like short rides, we have ice cream rides, cider and donut rides, and rides to see animals.

The annual Retired Senior Volunteer Recognition is always a big event, and a special trip. We have twenty-three R.S.V.P. volunteers, of which eighteen are residents.

A new outreach project should be challenging. Twenty miles away we have a subsidized housing project for elderly and handicapped people. There are thirty-eight people ranging in age from seventy-five to eighty-five years, who live there, and two-thirds of these people do not have transportation. Many of them have little or no social contact, outside of visiting with a neighbor.

I have asked if they would like to have some of our residents come up every so often to put on some sort of an activity like bingo, exercise class, sing-along, slide show or movie and we could even bring refreshments. That idea was warmly received and I have some residents who can't wait to go up there. Who knows what this project will lead to?

Judy continued,

Some residents would not ride in our station wagon because it had a state seal (labeling them). Our new bus has no state seal on it and it is not the state green color. The bus trips foster independence in the following way. All participants are free to:

- pick the trips they want to go on
- be able to request certain trips
- be able to sit where they want in restaurants, and with whom they want
- pay for their meals and handle and budget their own money
- choose clothing and other purchases, which has also resulted in an interest in proper dress

Trips have fostered a good feeling of being able to go into the community like anyone else and be treated like anyone else—a sense of belonging and community acceptance. Residents are made to feel better about themselves.

Accessory Apartments

The Minnesota Housing Finance Agency's Information Officer, Heidi Whitney, portrayed the Accessory Apartment program as follows:

Financing was made available through the sale of tax-exempt revenue bonds, setting aside approximately $1 million. An accessory apartment is a self-contained rental unit (with cooking, sleeping, and bathroom facilities) created within a house originally designed as a single-family dwelling. It was perceived that the child of an elderly parent who occasionally needed help, but who wanted to maintain privacy and independence would find this concept appealing. Also, a retired homeowner who wanted to travel, but was afraid to leave his home unattended, might be interested in remodeling.

Qualifications—You must own and occupy the property as your principal residence. The community must be participating in the program, and all necessary local permits obtainable. You must have a good credit history. The completed apartment must be in compliance with the State's Energy Code for Rental Housing. The interest is based on your annual adjusted income. A loan of $12,000 at 11½% rate with 180 monthly installments costs $140.28/month—no down payment.

Energy Conservation

Patricia Harris described the Tennessee Valley Authority (TVA) plan to conserve energy:

> Although our programs are available for all consumers, we are aware of the special problems of the elderly. We are working with Tennessee Green Thumb, an older American funded program, and have established a peer counseling program designed to help older Americans cope with energy-related problems. The peer counselors are older Americans trained on energy conservation by TVA. Then, they work one-on-one in their communities to reach older Americans with energy-related information. Through this program, over 84,000 consumers have been called, resulting in about 12,000 energy audits being conducted and about 11,000 homes being weatherized.
>
> Another example of TVA involvement with helping elderly residents meet the increased cost of energy is Project 2000. This began as a weatherization and carpentry training project to train high school students. While providing the training, the project also provided basic weatherization for elderly and disabled consumers. Over 1,000 households have been weatherized through this project, which is sponsored by local businesses, social service agencies, religious organizations, TVA, and the local power distributors.

Home Equity

The County of Nassau (NY) Department of Senior Citizen Affairs developed a program to allow seniors to borrow money against the equity they have in their homes. The initial payment can be used for renovations, repairs, payment of loans or taxes, purchase of equipment or in-home services. The regular monthly payments provide a supplement to fixed monthly income. For example: Mrs. L. is an eighty-four-year-old widow living in her own home with her sixty-five-year-old son. She has resided there for fifty-four years. Her only income is a monthly Social Security check plus some occasional food money from her son. Her basic home expenses include homeowner's insurance, property, and village taxes, utilities, water and fuel oil. She is in arrears on her fuel oil bill. In order to maintain herself, she has secured two bank loans. Her financial disbursements for household expenses and loan payments leave her a total of $6/month to spend for food, medicine and other unexpected expenses.

Mrs. L.'s only asset is her home. She has no money for a burial fund, which is a concern of her son, who is a severe diabetic and can only work sporadically. A home equity loan would enable Mrs. L. to pay off outstanding debts and put some money away for emergencies.

Doris Russell, Director, Division of Community Development Bureau for Maine's Elderly, stated,

> The option for asset-rich/cash-poor elderly has been to sell their home and move into less costly residences, or remain and face increasingly unaffordable taxes, insurance and maintenance expenses which, if not met, can force homes to depreciate in value. Home equity conversions provide the elderly with more options.
>
> There are several types of home equity conversion plans. In some, you will take out a loan, which will need to be repaid at your death, or when you decide to sell your home. Another model requires you to sell your home in exchange for lifetime residency and help with income and maintenance.

Trish Riley, Director of the Bureau of Medical Services, Maine, asserted,

> To our surprise, older people were more interested in financial independence than in passing on their estates to children. We also heard significant interest in a product design which we created, but did not see realized. The equity builder provides a fixed amount of loan, which an older person could take annually and the loan would be paid back at the person's death. Older people hesitated to take out home equity conversion loans because of the effect of compounding interest and the risk of indebtedness.

It would seem that home equity conversion and other options for shelter should be discussed with family members and with professionals in the field.

Suggestion

1 Change your home environment to make self-care easier.

maintaining independence in people with health problems

nursing care and maintaining function

Your elderly relative has been ill and hospitalized. Now he has been discharged to live with you, until he has regained his strength. The hospital nurse will teach you how to give necessary care to your elderly relative—insulin injections, dressing changes, etc. If possible, a home health nurse should come into your home and show you how to adapt what you learned in the hospital to fit into your home situation.

If you are a family member, then you will be allowed to do more for your patient than a non-family member being paid as a nurse's aide. Find out what the legal implications are in your state for the level of care that you are giving. What if you gave an injection, and later the person complained of a weakness in that leg? Long-term family feuds have been initiated with less provocation than that. What if you are a registered nurse, but you have been selling real estate for the last twenty years and are not up-to-date on current nursing practice? Even if you volunteer your services, you would still be held to the standard of practice of a registered nurse. I am not suggesting that you should not help out your friends, but use your common sense.

An acquaintance of mine who has a master's degree in nursing education came to me asking for tips on how to give intravenous chemotherapy injections to her neighbor. Her clinical skills were rusty and she was afraid of these toxic drugs infiltrating out of the vein and into surrounding tissue, causing tissue damage. She had never given an intravenous injection, but was embarrassed to tell her neighbor that. I strongly advised her to go to a workshop on how to give chemotherapy in the home, and practice this skill under supervision before attempting to give intravenous injections to her neighbor. In working with the elderly, one has to be especially careful, since their veins are not in good condition. It is hard to find a vein, and even when you have an intravenous infusion running that you can add drugs to, often the vein becomes inflamed after a couple of days of drug therapy, and you are back to step 1 again, looking for a vein.

So that you follow the physician's orders accurately, ask that they be written down. Also, ask that the nurse's instructions be written down or put on a cassette, so that you can refer back to the instructions. If you do not understand the instructions, ask for a clear explanation of them. You and your elderly relative will be under stress, and liable to forget what you have been taught to do. Don't hesitate to call the hospital or doctor for information.

In addition to carrying out instructions for care pertaining to the person's current acute health problem, you also need to carry out instructions on how to assist your relative in managing his chronic health problems. Look at what needs to be done, and develop a daily plan and weekly plan for giving care. Cluster client activities together before and after work, if you work outside the home. Ask the nurse for help in setting priorities for bathing, bedmaking, toileting and food. An elderly person does not need a complete bath every day. If you don't work outside the home, you should still arrange for someone to stay with your relative daily for a couple of hours, so that you can rest and participate in your normal social activities, particularly if the caregiver relationship is going to be maintained on a long-term basis. "Respite Care" is the term used for giving family time off from caregiving.

Try to make your daily schedule reflect your normal lifestyle as much as possible. For example, if your usual routine looks like this:

7:30 a.m.	Wash up before breakfast
8:00 a.m.	Eat breakfast and go to work
5:30 p.m.	Return home and make supper
6:00 p.m.	Eat supper
10:00 p.m.	Get ready for bed

then, you can get up one half hour earlier, and assist your patient with a partial bath, toileting and breakfast. If necessary, arrange for someone to come in for lunch and perhaps a walk outside. A bath and other care can be done after supper. Housework and laundry can be put off until the weekend. This is a heavy schedule. But it is difficult for middle-aged people who are paying off a house or college expenses to quit work and care full-time for a sick person at home, or alternatively pay $2,500/month for nursing home care.

The Chart—Buy a notebook and keep a record of your relative's condition. Divide the notebook into sections:

(1) Temperature, pulse, respirations, and blood pressure
(2) Intake and output
(3) Medications taken—date, time, and dosage
(4) Treatments given and patient's response
(5) Observations of patient

Write this information in black ink and do not erase or cross out. In this way, you will have documentation that you have given good care to your patient.

Suppose that an emergency occurs. You should become certified in cardiopulmonary resuscitation (CPR) and know how to contact an emergency service. For less drastic problems, write down the changes in the patient's condition and what you have done to try to solve the problem. Write down the instructions that the doctor gives you. Ask questions if you do not understand. Elderly people may have multiple chronic health problems. It is appropriate for health professionals to move from the medical model to an educational model, where families are taught to take care of themselves and keep control of their lives, as much as possible.

Observations

It is important to learn how to observe for signs and symptoms of health problems. Ask your doctor what the normal range for your elderly relative should be, for these observations. See him on a regular basis for health check-ups so that he can identify potential problems and solve them.

People have needs that are physical and safety-oriented. They also have needs for love, esteem and self-actualization. According to psychologist Abraham Maslow, a person's physical and safety needs have to be satisfied first, before a person can adequately meet his needs for love and esteem.

Here are some general observations you can make. A person will make additional specific observations depending upon his potential or actual health problems.

Circulatory and respiratory function

Blood pressure: check if elevated or too low.
Pulse: rate, strength, rhythm.
Temperature: check if elevated or too low, skin temperature in feet and hands, color, numbness, tingling, pain.
Respiration: rate, depth, rhythm, shortness of breath.
Changes in blood pressure, pulse and respiration when activity increased?
Does person smoke?
Productive or nonproductive cough: sputum production, frequency, color, amount.
Skin color changes? Bruising?
Effect of position on circulation and respiration.
Swelling of ankles.

Nutrition

Height, weight, fluid intake.
Mucous membranes: check if dry mouth, bleeding, gums decayed.
Type of diet, appetite, own teeth, denture fit, nausea.

Elimination

Bowel movement: frequency, amount, color, odor, diarrhea or constipation.
Chronic use of laxatives or enemas?
Urine: frequency, volume, color, odor, retention, incontinence, pain, difficulty in urinating.

Rest, activity, exercise

Sleeping adequate amount of time?
Factors disrupting sleep?
Presence of pain: onset-time, manner (gradual or sudden), precipitating factors. Characteristics of pain: quality, location, duration, timing (continuous or intermittent).
Complete bed rest or up and about?
Movement restricted: pain, stiffness, swelling around joints, shaking limbs or body, slowness in reacting, twitching.

Safety

Person needs assistance in moving.
Integrity of mucous membranes: sores, bumps.
Vision adequate?
Hearing adequate?
Anxiety about: surgery, therapeutic procedures, hospitalization, illness.
Behavior: depressed, abusive, angry, irritable, listless.
Economic security: paying for hospitalization, illness requiring change in or loss of job, concerns regarding financial future.

Love

Companionship of significant others?
Pleasant, helpful relationship with nurse, doctor, and other members of the
  health team.
Visitors present, photographs.

Esteem, self-esteem

Feels useful.
Maintains dignity.
Makes decisions.
Active participation in care.
Maintains as much independence as possible.

Self-actualization

Expresses creativity, need for truth, spiritual growth.

Activities of Daily Living

Daily necessities of self-care are referred to as activities of daily living (ADL). Knowledge of the level of function of each individual is essential for a successful ADL program. Here are basic self-care activities (ADL) developed by the Public Health Nursing Division of the
Colorado State Department of Public Health. (I have shortened the examples list.)

Bed activities

Moving from side to side
Turning over on to abdomen
Turning from sitting position to position with feet on floor, sitting on the side
  of the bed
Rolling from side to side
Rising from reclining to sitting

Personal hygiene

Caring for fingernails   Washing hands and face
Caring for teeth (dentures)   Shaving
Applying cosmetics   Combing hair
Bathing (bed, tub, shower)

Dressing and undressing

Putting on or removing—night clothes, underwear, shoes and socks, girdles, ty-
ing ties, shoe laces, buttoned clothing

Eating

Cutting meat
Paring or peeling vegetables
Using different utensils

Drinking (glass or cup)
Use of straw

Hand activities

Writing
Sewing
Dusting or cleaning rooms

Using telephone (holding receiver)
Making beds
Turning lights on and off

Wheelchair activities

Moving from bed to wheelchair and reverse
Moving from wheelchair to: toilet seat, tub, shower stool
Rising from wheelchair to standing
Propelling wheelchair: on level and on ramps (angle of ramp)
Locking wheelchair brakes

Walking

Moving from bed to standing
Rising from wheelchair to standing
Using cane, crutches, walkers, etc.

Walking on rough surfaces
Loss of balance
Climbing stairs

For more information about assessing and maintaining function, write to the U.S. government for the booklet *Elementary Rehabilitation Nursing Care*.

Relatives may note that there is a difference between how well an elderly person functions in a doctor's office or in a physical therapy department, and how well he functions at home. If the elderly person does not talk to the doctor much, a family member can report his own observations of the elder's behavior at home. An elderly person may work up to his full physical potential in the physical therapy department, and then sit around at home, being waited on by his wife.

A family member should accompany an elderly person to office visits and outpatient visits, if at all possible. Ask the nurse, physical therapist, or other health team member for advice on how to work with the elderly person at home. If there is a definite problem in transferring knowledge from the hospital to the home, it would be advisable to have a home health nurse work with the family and show them how to take care of the elderly person. It may be necessary to purchase a hospital bed, so that the caregiver will not injure her back bending over a low bed. On the other hand, before purchasing expensive equipment, find out if management of the elderly person's care at home is a reasonable objective.

Basic Skills

Environment

A clean, quiet environment facilitates recovery from illness. Reduce noise to promote rest. Smoking in bed may start a fire, unless a family member is present to monitor it. Of course, it is preferable not to smoke, but removing all cigarettes from the house of a heavy smoker is an action which will be strongly resented. Persuasion is better than emphasizing the person's weakness. In the event of a fire, how would the person in bed be taken out of the house? Is there a smoke detector in your home?

Good ventilation

Keep people with colds away from anyone recovering from illness. Clean and dust the environment regularly. After cleaning, return the person's possessions which he wants to keep near him.

Problems with immobility

A family member should receive instruction from a nurse and give a return demonstration in the home, before caring for a person with mobility problems. The caregiver needs to maintain good posture and body mechanics. Use the large thigh muscles for lifting, keeping the back straight. The caregiver may need to ask other family members or professionals for help. If necessary, a special mechanical patient lifter may be purchased.

A person confined to bed must be positioned properly to prevent joint deformity and muscle contractures. Body curves are supported with pillows or rolled towels. The position must be changed every hour to prevent pressure sores, where a bone close to the skin exerts pressure on the skin as the person lies on it.

Preventing infection

Body wastes and liquids can be disposed into the toilet. Use clean paper towels to pick up soiled tissues, dirty dressings, uneaten food, etc., and dispose in a plastic bag. Close the bag with ties and put outside in a closed garbage can. After a person uses a bedpan, empty it into the toilet and rinse with cold water. Clean the bedpan with soap and water and put away.

Elimination

Maintain a record of the person's normal pattern of elimination. Give the urinal and bedpan at regular intervals, and upon request. Encourage fluids and foods with fiber. If the person does not have enough urine output, or is showing symptoms of diarrhea or constipation, call your doctor for advice.

Bathing

A daily bath may not be necessary, since an older person has a tendency to have dry skin. Keep a bath blanket over the person to prevent chilling. Test the water temperature on the inner wrist, because your hands are used to hot water and you do not want to burn your relative. Your relative will probably be able to bathe himself, with some help in doing his back or feet. A person with an indwelling catheter should wash carefully with soap around the catheter. Clean dentures over a bowl of water to prevent breakage.

The New York State Office for the Aging has a book for family caregivers, *Practical Help*, which goes into details about basic skills needed by the caregiver. However, to give care to meet the specific needs of your relative, the best way is to have a nurse show you how to do it, and then do it yourself with supervision.

Maintaining Function

The fact that a person has limitation in certain areas does not rule out independence. Juanita Hagemeier, Acting Director of the Disabled Citizens Alliance for Independence, stated:

> There are several ways we promote independence, The most successful has been through crafts. Recreation has been a major catalyst to get elderly people involved in community affairs. Keep in mind we work with severely disabled people. The majority of our elderly people were able-bodied in their youth. Our young disabled give encouragement, support, acceptance, friendship, and genuine concern for their health and well-being. In turn, the elderly have much to give. Many of our most talented are our elderly. They teach (with patience) our young disabled. New friendships are developed.
>
> By coming together as a group, and as friends, they have accomplished the following: incorporating Partnerships on Disabilities, applied for and received their tax exempt status, raised funds, purchased a lift-equipped van, successfully lobbied for accessible housing, ap-

proached the county to be included in a mill tax levy to purchase a building for their use, and worked successfully toward passage of this levy. The Staff of DCAI have been involved, supplying transportation, moral support, and working alongside them to accomplish their goals.

A seventy-nine-year-old lady (mobility impaired) made this statement regarding the group: "You know, I spent a lot of nights and days by myself after my husband died, and now I don't know what it is to be lonesome anymore." Another elderly woman had this to say: "I've met so many nice people here. I really didn't know what I was missing, and I'm sorry I had to get disabled to find all of you people. It just seems like when I don't show up at these meetings, everybody misses me. I never had anyone miss me before. I kind of like it."

Our agency has a lift-equipped bus that is available for local trips, shopping, medical appointments, banking, etc. We also have an equipment loan program—walkers, wheelchairs, commodes, bath benches, reachers, etc., as well as a personal care and homemaker program we can put in place where needed. We encourage voter registration and offer transportation to the polls.

Being in a rural area, the majority of our elderly value their independence greatly, and do not hesitate accepting the help they may need to maintain that independence. DCAI is unique: we cover all disabilities, all ages, and have no income guidelines.

Jo Mach, Occupational Therapist, provided information about the "Living It Up" program of Topeka-Shawnee County Health Department, in which she and Joyce Gorsuch-Burns, M.S.W., were active. Mach stated:

Limitations on physical and mental independence lead to isolation, depression, and an increasing dependence on others. Some of these limiting factors are:

- lack of transportation
- lack of physical energy, strength, and mobility
- limited hearing or vision
- infrequent contact with family members
- reoccurring loss of friends due to death or illness
- increased expense and time related to health problems
- lack of role in community and family

The "Living It Up" program includes twelve different sessions to allow for discussion, teaching, and activities related to these factors. The program was held in apartments or meal sites with transportation provided. The program began each session with sitting exercises done to uplifting, fun music. One woman with multiple sclerosis confined to a wheelchair did what she was able to do. A day of overdoing can cause a week of not having energy. Pacing oneself and following your own rhythm was discussed. Time management concepts were taught, such as, resting periodically with your feet up as you tire during the day, and having a very easy day planned before and after a day of shopping or going to the doctor.

Many different illnesses are associated with diminished strength and mobility, for example, heart disease, arthritis, chronic obstructive pulmonary disease, stroke, and cancer. A person has to live with these illnesses for many years. There is adaptive equipment, such as reachers, long-handled shoehorns, jar openers, zipper pulls, button hooks, card holders, and many other things that can be helpful.

Infrequent contact with family members and loss of friends causes feelings of isolation. One session focused on reminiscing. Participants were encouraged to see that their life had been interesting and it was full of experiences worthy of being shared. Sharing these memories was a way of making new friends and also of experiencing some of those good feelings again. Life review is an important part of growing older, so it was encouraged.

The session on stress management provided the participants with a tool to use when dealing with sad and lonely times. Several techniques were taught, including face and shoulder massage, guided imagery, muscle relaxation, visualization, and deep breathing. By teaching many techniques participants were free to decide what worked best for them, and then were encouraged to put some of the techniques into their daily routine. Assertiveness training was initiated through role playing, and everyone was given a list of Assertive Bill of Rights. This helps elderly individuals reach for their independence.

A lack of role in the community and family is partly the fault of society, but through encouragement the elderly can learn to see their value as an individual, and to see how others need them to brighten their day. Often the participants didn't know the name of the person they sat across from at the table every noon, or the name of the person who lived across the hall. Through group involvement, the participants were able to get to know others, realize things they had in common, and feel good about making a new friend. At the conclusion of the sessions, each participant could be a resource to others outside the group, and also they had strengthened their socialization skills to allow for more reaching out to others.

Mentally, they were encouraged to be themselves and experience acceptance and friendship as a result of their sharing. By not restricting their thoughts to their problems, they allowed themselves to continue to grow through learning new ideas and meeting new people. Physically, participants were encouraged to exercise to the best of their ability, and were given tools to allow them to be more physically independent in their daily life. Some participants met new friends, who were willing to help them in daily activities, such as giving them a ride to the store or doing their grocery shopping for them.

Suggestions

1 Find out what nursing skills you need to have to become a caregiver for a family relative.
2 Enroll in a short course at your local community for nurse's aide education.

long-term use of medication

Physiological Changes and Drugs

According to the American Association of Colleges of Pharmacy, those over sixty-five years of age use more than twenty-five percent of all drugs prescribed, and this figure will increase as the percentage of elderly people over sixty-five increases. In one study of long-term care facilities, nearly thirty-two percent of all elderly patients received eight or more different medications daily, and some patients received as many as fifteen drugs. The elderly account for about sixty-nine percent of hospital discharges and about ninety percent of the long-term institutional care. Also, they are the recipients of as much as fifty percent of the total amount spent on health care.

As the aging process alters human physiology, drug metabolism is affected. Kidney function is reduced by as much as forty percent by the time a person reaches age ninety. This reduced rate of elimination may lead to an accumulation of drugs in the bloodstream that could be harmful. The action of a given drug may differ significantly in the elderly, compared to the younger adult. Average drug reactions for elderly patients increase with increasing age.

Elderly patients have decreased reserve related to each organ. However, not all organs age at the same time, so the brain may be functioning well, while the heart may be tired. Enzymes in the liver involved in breaking down drugs become less effective. Renal filtration of drugs is less effective. There is a decrease in pain sensation, which means that the elderly probably need lower doses of pain medication.

Polypharmacy means multiple drug use. Many elderly people have multiple health problems, requiring drug therapy. This increases the probability of drug interactions, and of side effects.

Murray Zarfes is Director of Pharmacy at the Daughters of Jacob Geriatric Center in New York. He relayed information about their Drug-Free Day program, stating that "the geriatric patient has a lower metabolic rate, and therefore a greater tendency for drug levels to accumulate in the body tissues, when prescribed for long-term therapy. The Drug-Free Day (DFD) was initiated after several lengthy meetings. By skipping medication one day a week, the program removes the slowly elevating amounts of drugs, along with their side effects.

"The patient's body has a chance to rest. The nurse has additional time to spend with the residents. There is a financial savings for the institution. The doctor is more receptive to lowering the dosage of the drugs, if the resident does well on the Drug-Free Day program."

Dr. Dennis Hyams, M.D., Senior Medical Director of Merck, Sharp & Dohme, suggests the following questions and principles of drug use in the elderly should be used as guidelines.

- Is the drug really necessary?
- Is the drug appropriate? (Has the diagnosis been established?)
- Will the drug make the patient worse than the illness? (What adverse reactions are likely?)
- Use a minimum number of drugs. (Establish priorities in each patient individually.)
- Use the simplest, minimal dosage regimen.
- Use a few drugs well.
- Add drugs to a regimen one at a time.
- Stop a drug when its effect is no longer required.
- Ensure appropriate presentation of drugs (format, route, packaging, labelling, education of patient and relatives).

Elderly people who are confused may mix the various drugs they have received over a period of time. Compliance with the drug regimen is difficult if the person does not understand the doctor's explanation. Child-proof containers may be too difficult for elderly people to open.

According to Dr. Hyams, "the aims of drug treatment in old age are:

- cure of disease
- amelioration of symptoms
- improvement in function of organs and of the whole person
- preservation of mentality, mobility and continence"

Several categories of drugs cause side effects in the elderly, in addition to the aims for which they were prescribed.

Cardiovascular Drugs

Digoxin toxicity is one of the most common drug reactions in the elderly, since the elderly need smaller doses than middle-aged adults, because of impaired renal function and low blood potassium level. Nausea, vomiting and slow heart rate do not present as symptoms of overdose as frequently as they present in the middle-aged. Heart failure, cardiac arrhythmias, and mental changes are more common side effects as the person ages. Hyams perceives that seventy percent of the elderly are probably on the wrong dose of digoxin.

Diuretics

These drugs should be prescribed only if really indicated. Swelling of the ankles is not always due to heart failure. Diuretics for edema can lead to incontinence due to urinating more frequently with a greater sense of urgency, or to limited mobility, if the person cannot make it to the toilet in time. These drugs can lead to a low blood volume, fluid and electrolyte imbalance, low blood pressure and shock. If necessary, the doctor will prescribe a potassium supplement for use with certain drugs which increase potassium loss. Diuretics and other drugs are sometimes prescribed for hypertension. If so, it is necessary to monitor the blood pressure carefully, so that enough blood reaches the brain and the person does not become dizzy due to low blood pressure.

Drug Education

The Care Assurance System for the Aging and Home Bound (CASA) is a volunteer ministry in Alabama. Here are some examples of people who received drug education from the program.

> Picture Mary. Her aged hands shake uncontrollably, yet barely noticeably, as she sits and watches children play outside her window. Her eyes sparkle but her sight is dim. She rises and walks carefully to her kitchen on schedule. Her hands reach for a small bottle, her eyes search for a clue that it is the right medication for 3 p.m., but the trembling hand and poor eyesight create fear for her as she checks other medicine containers. "What if this is the wrong one, or I take too many?" she wonders.
> And Daniel. His strong hands that created beautiful furniture in his garage carpentry shop are gnarled and curled with arthritis. He reaches

for his medication and fights the bottle, his hands and arms tense as he struggles and pain shoots through them to his shoulders. "Child-proof," he shouts, and tosses the bottle back on the shelf. Holding his hands cradled in his arms, he walks away.

And Minnie. By her bed is a table full of medication. She has been in and out of the hospital many times in the past few months. Diagnoses have changed, and so has her medication. Many bottles on her bedside table are outdated. Some hold medicine that is no longer prescribed. There are a few empty packages of sample medicines the doctor just prescribed but Minnie has never had filled. She weeps softly as she studies her bedside table and takes the "normal" doses—some old, some new. She can't afford to throw away the old medicine, and can't afford to buy the new.

Each of us knows the difficulty of remembering to take medicines, of juggling several and remembering what to take when. For persons with handicapping conditions—loss of sight, aged hands, loss of mobility, and so many others—these problems which we can solve quickly are frightening and even painful.

The Med CO/OP program is designed to provide a method for these people to set up multiple medications on a convenient yet safe schedule of intake. Each program is individually designed by a volunteer in the home with the caretaker, and with the knowledge and help of the physician and pharmacist. Clients come to us by physician referral only, and volunteers coordinate a series of visits to teach the client and primary caretaker how to organize the medications for easy intake. Evaluations are made by a participating pharmacist to determine any dangers with the multiple medications and multiple-physician client. Our hope is to be an advocate for safety, and agent of support for persons who cannot or do not take medications properly.

Jacquelyn Nowak, Director of Bureau of Advocacy, described the Drug Education Program of the Department of Aging, Harrisburg, PA:

Senior citizens use twenty-five percent of all medications. More than thirty-one percent of all senior citizens experience adverse drug reactions. In Pennsylvania, that equates to more than 700,000 people.

Twenty-three percent of nursing home admissions can be attributed primarily to patients' inability to manage their medications at home. More than sixty percent of all patient visits to a physician result in a prescription. Use of over-the-counter drugs outnumbers prescriptions by a 3 to 2 ratio. Prescription drugs are twice as expensive.

Seventy percent of all women use at least one over-the-counter drug. A majority of the elderly use over-the-counter drugs, but that use declines to below the national average as people turn more to prescription drugs after the age of sixty-five. Adverse drug reactions rank seventh among causes for hospital admission, and result in annual hospitalization costs of $4.5 billion.

In response to a need for senior citizens to control their own well-being through proper use of prescription medications and over-the-counter drugs, three Pennsylvania organizations developed the "Medication Passport." The sponsoring groups are the Pennsylvania Department of Aging, the Pennsylvania Pharmaceutical Association and the Blue Cross and Blue Shield Plans of Pennsylvania.

The key to the program is the recognition that there are three major roles to be played in preventing adverse drug reactions: those of the patient, the physician and the pharmacist. The Passport is intended to serve as a common communications tool, through which each will record or double check the various prescriptions and over-the-counter drugs used by senior citizens.

A basic difficulty in administering medication to the elderly is the inability to carry out foolproof drug testing among the elderly. Varied lifestyles, chronic illness, body experiences, and biological changes make it extremely difficult to test drugs among the elderly. And worse, such testing can actually put a senior citizen at risk.

Older people must receive individualized treatment, attention and monitoring. Each person can react differently to a single drug, or a combination of drugs. Drugs tend to seek out adipose or fatty tissue, of which older people have disproportionate amounts. Therefore, prescribed doses can be ineffective or unpredictable. Many drugs "bind" to blood protein, leaving a lesser amount of free active drug in the blood. However, serum albumin declines among older persons, thereby releasing more unbound active drug in, again, an unpredictable manner.

There are more than 2600 drugs and drug families, but only 200 of those or eight percent account for two-thirds of all prescriptions. Among senior citizens, the most frequently used medications are: antiarthritic medications and agents, analgesics, diuretics, tranquilizers, sedatives, antibiotics and cardiovascular drugs. Tranquilizers and sedatives dominate prescriptions for patients' non-specific complaints. Diuretics and cardiovascular medications dominate treatment for disease-specific complaints.

The two most frequently purchased over-the-counter drugs are aspirin and vitamins. Non-aspirin analgesics and cough and cold preparations follow as most frequently purchased. The same group continues to be popular among senior citizens, but the two most frequently purchased over-the-counter drugs are laxatives and antacid preparations. There are a number of reasons adverse drug reaction occurs increasingly among the elderly:

- the increased likelihood of chronic illness
- the increase in drug use
- the increased likelihood of reaction to high-potential drugs used to treat specific diseases
- habitual use of over-the-counter, self-care drugs and lack of recognition that newly prescribed drugs may interact

- physiological changes which reduce the body's ability to discharge excess drugs
- a general slowing of body response to stress within the system

Beyond drug-to-drug and drug-to-food reactions, the potential exists for drug-to-alcohol reactions. It is not necessary for an older person to abuse alcohol to experience an adverse reaction.

Apparent signs and symptoms lead to a medical diagnosis and drug therapy. However, in the elderly, diseases may manifest themselves with signs and symptoms that are different from those apparent in middle-aged people with the same disease. As a consequence, people may receive a medical diagnosis and drug therapy which do not match the actual disease.

Non-compliance is a complex problem. Factors predisposing to this include:

- Chronic illnesses and physical impairments lead to less compliance.
- The length of the physician's regime and multiple drugs result in less compliance.
- A worsening illness, less stable economic status, and being alone lead to less compliance.
- Self-care and self-diagnosis can result in a decision to not comply with a doctor's instructions.

Under Pennsylvania Pharmaceutical Assistance Contract for the Elderly (PACE) older persons spent an average of $207 a year on 18 prescriptions. The average cost of these prescriptions is $11.50 each. A group of 4 million senior citizens spends upward to $250 and beyond each year on their medications.

Here are some tips from the Pennsylvania Department of Aging. Ask yourself:

- Do I take medication on time?
- Do I take the correct amount?
- Do I stop taking it too soon?
- Do I mix it with alcohol? Food? Other medications?
- Do I inform my doctor of all medications I am taking?

Ask your doctor:

- What is the name of the medication?
- Why am I taking it?
- How often should I take it?

- How long must I take it?
- Is there a generic (not a brand name) equivalent right for me?
- Will the instructions be given in writing?
- Are there any side effects?

Before your doctor visit make a list of any questions you have and a list of all medications you are taking. Then you will not forget to ask any question important to you. Also, it will save time for both you and your doctor.

Ask your pharmacist:

- Can you provide easy-to-open containers?
- Will you type the label in large print?
- Do you keep a list of all prescriptions you fill for me?
- What do I do if I miss a dose?
- Will over-the-counter medications interact?
- What other cautions should I observe?

The following is a Medication Calendar from the Health Information Services of Merck, Sharp & Dohme. The first six columns are descriptive.

Name of medicine   Color/shape   Take with   Do not take with

1. _____

How much   Times to take   S   M   T   W   Th   F   S

Note under "Take with" whether to take on an empty stomach or with food or milk. For "Do not take with" note foods, medicines or alcohol, that you do not want to take with this medication. List specific "Times to take"—8 a.m., 6 p.m.—not just "two times daily." Place a check in the correct box—Sunday, etc.—after you take each dose of medicine, to have a record of one week's medications taken, after the columns have been completed.

Drug Storage

Merck's Health Information Services states that correct storage of medicine is essential to maintain its potency and safety. They offer the following guidelines:

(1) Do not store medicines in the medicine cabinet in your bathroom or in the kitchen; the humidity can harm them.
(2) Keep medicines well out of children's reach. If there are no

children living in the home and you have arthritis, ask the pharmacist to give you medication with an ordinary cap, not child-proof, but be sure to keep medication in a place that visiting children cannot reach.

(3) Store all medicines in their original containers, with labels securely attached. Some medicines must remain packaged in dark glass, or solid white plastic, to protect their potency.

(4) Never combine different tablets or capsules in the same container. Follow this rule also when packing medicine for a trip; if necessary, ask your pharmacist for small containers to carry your medicines safely.

(5) Don't put medicines in the glove compartment of the car, in the sun or on window sills. Excessive heat or cold can affect the ingredients.

Use of Media

Your community group could become involved in drug education using the radio. The National Safety Council suggests using the following script or similar material.

EXPIRED PRESCRIPTIONS

A. 30-SECOND RADIO SPOT
With food prices what they are these days, it makes sense to save your leftovers. But you should never save outdated medicine. Prescription medicine's effectiveness can change over time. Some can even become harmful. And when your cabinet is cluttered with prescriptions you're no longer taking, it's easier to mistake one medicine for another. Clean out your medicine cabinet regularly to keep it safe. And keep your leftovers in the kitchen. A public service message from the National Safety Council and _____ (station).

B. 15-SECOND RADIO SPOT
With food prices what they are these days, it makes sense to save all your leftovers. But you should never save outdated medicine. Medicine's effectiveness can change over time. Clean out your medicine cabinet and keep it safe. A public service message from the National Safety Council and _____ (station).

PRESCRIPTIONS ARE PERSONAL

A. 30-SECOND RADIO SPOT
You have a bad backache and you want relief immediately. . . . Is it all right

to take the pain relieving medication the doctor prescribed for another member of your family? The answer is no. Doctors prescribe medication for a patient's specific problem, so it can be dangerous to take someone else's medication. It is important to consult the doctor yourself. All prescriptions are personal. To protect your family, clean out your medicine cabinet regularly. A public service message from the National Safety Council and _____ (station).

B. 15-SECOND RADIO SPOT
If you get sick, is it all right to take medication prescribed for someone else? The answer is no. All prescriptions are personal. Consult the doctor yourself. To protect your family, clean out your medicine cabinet regularly. A public service message from the National Safety Council and _____ (station).

The National Association of Retail Druggists in association with Lilly has developed drug education slides and audiocassettes, to show to community groups. "What You Don't Know About Drugs Can Hurt You!" runs about twelve minutes and describes problems that people encounter with medicines, such as drug interactions or side effects, or may cause themselves by administering drugs improperly. It also stresses the need for proper understanding and use of medicines. "Drug Abuse: What, Who, How, and Why and Strategies for Prevention and Treatment" runs about twelve minutes and describes problems associated with abuse of both illicit and legal drugs.

The Quack

If orthodox medicine cannot cure a person's illness, it is only natural that desperate people will spend a lot of money on alternative health treatments, which may or may not alleviate their distress. Roger Miller is editor of the U.S. government journal *FDA Consumer* from the Food and Drug Administration. Miller observed that quackery thrives because the quack exploits people's desire for cures for their ills, and he knows how to advertise using mysticism, pseudoscience, and sensationalism. For example, "An amazing breakthrough in medical technology" has resulted in a product that "reverses hereditary pattern baldness." Or "clinical studies prove that" you really can stop the aging process. These sound like major scientific milestones.

Today's medicine man is not above using the exotic in his promotion pieces. Indeed, sometimes he even combines the foreign with the scientific, as in "now from Europe comes a remarkable skin care break-through: cell therapy." Quack products today are all "natural," "100 per-cent natural ingredients" and "works safe and naturally," and "nature wants you to function perfectly."

But if Mother Nature and scientists are working feverishly to restore your health or youth, your diet is what's killing you, as these lines at-test: "Modern diets are poor in nutrition." "Modern food processing strips away many key nutrients from our diets." "Most people do not manage to eat a well balanced diet."

Here is an alphabetized list of quackery terms developed by Roger Miller and taken from his *FDA Consumer* article, "The Voice of the Quack."

Quack Language from A to Z

A = Amazing (as in "amazing breakthrough")

B = Breakthrough

C = Clinical

D = Discovery, doctor (as in "Doctor makes amazing discovery")

E = Exciting, European, enzymes (as in "This exciting European discovery of new enzymes resulted from an amazing clinical breakthrough.")

F = Fantastic (as in "'It was fantastic; within 3 weeks the pain had left,' writes Mrs. Z. B. of Chatsworth, Calif."); also, formula, fast-working.

G = Guaranteed

H = Home cure (as in "Now there's an amazing home cure for arthritis, thanks to a fantastic scientific breakthrough accom-plished in a Finnish laboratory.")

I = Instant, immediate, inexpensive, ingredient

J = Just (as in "'The pain was gone in just 3 weeks,' reports B. Z. of Bellflower, Ill.")

K = Know-how (as in "With a special brand of understanding and know-how, Dr. Strange was able to come up with this secret formula.")

L = Lose (as in "guaranteed to lose 3 pounds a night while you sleep.")

M = Medical (also "medically approved," "medical technology"); also "miracle" and "miraculous"

N = Natural (as in "Now there's a natural way to lose those excess pounds."); may also be used in the French form "naturel"; also "nutrients" (as in "Your normal diet doesn't provide the proper nutrients.")

O = On the spot (as in "Feel the texture of your hair change on the spot to silken smoothness.")

P = Painless

Q = Quick

R = Research, researcher, revolutionize (as in "revolutionize the process of preventing baldness"); also remarkable (as in "_____ is a remarkable scientific discovery.")

S = Secret, speed, safe

T = Technology

U = Uncover (as in "researchers uncover secret formula")

V = Vanish (as in "liver spots vanish miraculously")

W = Wonder, works (as in "It really works.")

X = X rays (as in "X rays prove that arthritic calcium deposits are cleared up.")

Y = Youthful

Z = Zinc (as in "The mineral crucial to man's prowess.")

As Miller states, "The real harm comes, however, because people rely on the quack's product, when they probably should be seeing a physician. On the other hand, if traditional medicine cannot cure or help a person with his health problems, and the person believes that a pill or ointment will help him, he is going to buy that pill or ointment. Also, what is quackery?"

Years ago acupuncture was commonly regarded by the public as quackery. Now there are acupuncture clinics affiliated with hospitals and run by medical doctors. I have tried acupuncture once for a health problem and it did not help me at all. However, certain people have had good results with pain relief, after intensive acupuncture treatments. It would seem that we need more research to find cures for cancer and other illnesses and to find out which therapeutic regimes really help patients.

Suggestions

1 If your elderly relative takes a lot of medications, buy a resource drug book. For example, *About Your Medications*, available from

the U.S. Pharmacopoeia, 12601 Twinbrook Parkway, Maryland, contains important information. The format used is:

- medication brand and generic names
- before using this medication . . .
- proper use of this medication
- precautions while using this medication
- side effects of this medication

2 <u>Practitioner Reporting</u>: Practitioner Reporting System (800) 638-6725, (301)881-0256 in Maryland (call collect). Whenever you have a problem with a drug or medical device, tell your physician or nurse. The above system offers a service for health professionals to report these problems. A service of the Food and Drug Administration, U.S. Department of Health and Human Services.

cardiovascular and respiratory problems

Peripheral Vascular Disease

Obstruction of normal circulation in blood vessels of the arms and legs causing lack of oxygenation and pain is referred to as peripheral vascular disease. Loss of elasticity of the blood vessel walls and fatty deposits on the inside of the walls lead to slower circulation of the blood. This facilitates blood clot formation. Pain in the calf muscles after walking or exercise, which goes away with rest, is called intermittent claudication. It is a sign of poor arterial circulation. If pain occurs when the person is resting, then the person has a severe form of diminished circulation.

Poor venous circulation leads to swelling of the ankles with retained fluid. The legs feel heavy and the skin may be warm and reddened by the end of the day. Pain in the calf may indicate an inflammation in the veins, which could lead to a blood clot formation, interfering with blood circulation back to the heart.

The major potential problem of clots is that part of the clot could become dislodged into the circulation as an embolism. It will obstruct blood circulation wherever it lodges. A pulmonary embolism is manifested by chest pain, shortness of breath, and a rapid pulse rate. This complication requires immediate medical attention. Oxygen and anticoagulation therapy are usually ordered.

A program of prescribed exercise improves circulation, since the contraction of the calf muscles acts like a second heart pumping the circulation. Elevation of the feet when sitting improves venous circulation, whereas lowering the feet improves arterial circulation. Obesity places more strain on the circulation, because the extra fat needs more blood vessels to provide nourishment. An obese person will be advised to lose weight.

Redness, heat, and pain in the calf indicate inflammation of a blood vessel, with the potential for clot formation and embolism. Bed rest with the affected leg elevated is required. Anticoagulants will prevent the spread of the clotting. The person has to be monitored for further clotting and also for hemorrhage, shown by blood in the urine, bleeding from the nose, etc., and bruising of the skin. Either complication would necessitate a change in drug dosage.

The American Heart Association has a booklet, *An Older Person's Guide to Cardiovascular Health*, which offers information about the signs and symptoms of cardiovascular problems and suggests problem-solving actions. The American Heart Association offers CPR classes on a regular basis in the community. Everyone should consider becoming CPR certified, so that he or she could save the life of someone having a heart attack.

Angina

When the coronary artery is not supplying enough blood to the heart, a pain is felt in the heart muscle: angina. Pain should be investigated by a physician, to find out if the person has had a heart attack, causing cell death to the heart muscle. If the physician diagnoses angina, then he may recommend surgery to increase the blood supply to the heart muscle—bypassing the blocked artery. If the chest pain is mild angina, which is not causing permanent damage, then the physician may prescribe the following more conservative measures:

- balancing rest and activity to prevent tiring the heart
- staying on prescribed diet
- no smoking
- avoiding stress

Congestive Heart Failure

The aging heart muscle may not have the strength to increase cardiac output when necessary, due to increased physical activity. The person becomes fatigued more easily, demonstrates shortness of breath when exercising, has a cough and swollen ankles. Chest pain may not be present. These symptoms occur when the heart does not contract strongly enough to empty and fluid backs up into the lungs and later causes congestion in the systemic circulation—a condition known as congestive heart failure. This may occur as a result of a heart attack, which scars the heart muscle so it cannot pump efficiently.

The person with a heart problem needs to monitor his signs and symptoms and report changes to his doctor. An exercise regime will be ordered, which maintains activity within the limits of the heart's ability to deliver oxygen and nutrients to the body's tissues. Continuous flow oxygen may be necessary, to ensure adequate oxygenation of the tissues.

Digitalis medication may be prescribed to strengthen the contraction ability of the heart. A failing heart does not have the strength to handle a fluid overload. Various measures help to decrease fluid retention: a low sodium diet; diuretics to increase urine output; and digitalis to increase the blood flow to the kidneys, thus promoting greater urine output. To monitor fluid retention by the tissues, the intake and output of fluids is measured, and the person is weighed before breakfast in the same clothing daily.

Stroke

The narrowing or complete closing of one of the blood vessels of the brain, which reduces its blood flow, is called a cerebrovascular accident or stroke. It can be caused by a blood clot, embolism, or hemorrhage from a ruptured blood vessel. Factors which increase the risk of developing stroke include hypertension and diabetes. An elevated blood pressure in combination with any weakness in an artery may lead to a ruptured blood vessel and cerebral hemorrhage. Diabetes is associated with fatty deposits in the walls of blood vessels, which narrows the diameter of the vessels, slows the circulation, and leads to blood clots and inadequate circulation.

To prevent stroke a person needs to be aware of the warning signs of a stroke. Transient ischemic attack is a temporary lack of blood supply to the brain due to the spasm of a narrowed cerebral artery. The signs and symptoms of this attack are temporary and do not leave any residual permanent effects. The most common are: numbness, tingling or weakness in an arm, leg, or one side of the face; blindness; speech difficulty; loss of strength in a limb. Less common signs are headache, dizziness, or confusion. Contact a physician. It is possible to perform surgery to clear out the fatty plaques in the cerebral artery, and improve the blood supply to prevent a stroke. Bypass surgery reroutes blood past an obstruction in a blood vessel.

Stroke affects intellect, emotion, communication, and personality. Half the victims of stroke with a paralysis on the right side develop aphasia, that is, difficulty in speaking or in understanding speech. The family may be anxious, may feel guilty, and may be unrealistic in setting rehabilitation goals, because they do not understand what is happening to their relative. Speech therapy may help the person to communicate more effectively with her relatives, through use of gestures, pictures, and pointing to letters on a word board, in addition to other methods.

A person who has a left-sided paralysis is more likely to have perceptual disturbances. She has difficulty with spatial relationships, for example, knowing where paralyzed limbs are located. A person may run her wheelchair over her paralyzed foot, and she will not feel it. She needs to be taught to look and check where her limbs are located. Sometimes a sling is worn, or a leg may be restrained by ties, so that it will not fall off the wheelchair and be injured.

If conscious on admission to the hospital, a person who has had a stroke has a better chance of survival than if unconscious. Stroke is the third leading cause of death after heart disease and cancer. A rehabilitation plan should start within 48 hours after admission. Most recovery occurs in 4–6 months, if it is going to happen.

Steven Miner sent me information about Burke Rehabilitation Center in White Plains, NY, which provides rehabilitation to assist people to gain maximum levels of independence, in activities of daily living, communication, gait, ability to use public transportaion and facilities, and to be independent at home. The program includes:

- general conditioning exercises
- activities of daily living
- homemaking evaluation and programs
- perceptual evaluation and training
- functional speech/language and communication
- trips
- equipment evaluation and recommendations
- home visits to evaluate necessary modifications
- programs to educate the patient and family about managing the patient at home

Judith Fox, Administrator, described the Hilo Adult Day Care Center program to help people who have had a stroke and their families. The Hawaiian name for the organization is "Hale Kupuna," House of Grandparents. This organization is private, nonprofit, and receives its referrals from physicians, the hospital, public health workers, and private families. Fox stressed that "preventative health is emphasized and we monitor weight and blood pressure on a monthly basis. Dramatic fluctuations are reported to the families and the client's physician." She continued:

> Our program runs from 7:00 a.m. to 5:00 p.m. We provide a morning snack, a hot lunch (provided by Hawaii County Nutrition Program), and an afternoon snack. We offer a variety of services to our clients such as: physical therapy, exercise, nutrition education, occupational therapy, music therapy, reminiscent therapy, arts and crafts, ceramics, woodworking, consumer education, legal assistance, financial assistance, guidance and counselling, education from the community college. We have once-a-week required field trips. If it were not for the existence of our Center, most of our clients would be institutionalized.

A person with a stroke requires months of rehabilitation. He learns how to use his unaffected arm and leg to move his paralyzed arm and leg. Blood does not circulate well through the paralyzed limb, because there is no muscle movement to keep the circulation moving. It is easier to dress the affected side first. Clothes with front closure are easy to handle.

When bathing, the person can sit on a non-slip chair or stool and use a spray hose. If incontinence is a problem, then a condom-like external catheter drainage may help. When a person needs help during the day, or becomes lonely at home by himself, adult day care makes a difference in providing stimulation and companionship.

Billie Jo Lamaze, RN, described the rehabilitation program at Friendship House Adult Day Care Center in Alexandria, Louisiana:

> The program of promoting independence in the elderly participant is an ongoing and never ceasing integral plan of daily care. The focus is on wellness rather than illness, stressing preventive care and health maintenance. Instead of looking at infirmities, we point out the areas of functional abilities. We feel that by keeping the spirit uplifted, we will instill the desire not only to maintain but to restore.
>
> We have daily health checks including blood pressures and weights. We encourage total participant participation, regardless of the infirmities, in daily exercises. Done in groups there is always more involvement, more encouragement to keep up with the group . . . to excel. The stroke patient begins working more with the infirmed arm or leg.

They are taught to use the "good" hand or arm to move the paralyzed arm to keep the muscles firm. We see remarkable improvement in range of motion. We encourage movement of the infirmed leg, and in the exercises we do, they regain confidence of being able to put weight on the infirmed leg. One participant's wife stated that for the first time in years, her husband was able to get up and down from the curb in front of their house. One of our ladies reported that she could once again help with dish-washing in the home. The staff works not only with participants and their families, but with the physician, physiotherapists and speech therapists to keep the recommended regimen on a daily basis.

Friendship House also cares for the Alzheimer's and Parkinson's disease participant, organic brain syndrome, and withdrawn, socially reclusive persons. With some participants it can never be restorative, but with encouragement and strong family counseling and support, it can be hopefully maintained for a long period of time.

With transition into Friendship House, the groundwork can be started for a much less traumatic transfer into a nursing home, when that time does come. Working with the family members, much of the stress is alleviated, and the ultimate result of the nursing home placement can be made knowing that everything that could be done was done, making this change more easily accepted. We have never had to take the initiative to start nursing home placement proceedings. The family home situation resolves this problem in a natural course as the participant becomes more dependent. It becomes impossible for the participant to remain in a family situation without professional help through the nights and over weekends.

We remain supportive and help the families through this transitional period of time. Being available for participants and families, giving them support, care, and understanding is what Friendship House is all about.

Chronic Obstructive Pulmonary Disease

This disease process interferes with the lungs' ability to breathe. Asthma, bronchitis, and emphysema lead to chronic obstructive pulmonary disease (COPD), since they obstruct the bronchi. Asthma is an attack of shortness of breath and wheezing. An allergic stimulus causes the bronchi to go into a spasm in an attempt to prevent this substance from entering the body through the lungs. This reaction is actually protective in nature, but the result is not satisfactory since it interferes with ventilation. Elimination of the allergic stimulus or desensitization will prevent the bronchial spasm from occurring. If it is not possible to use this approach, then steroid medication is sometimes used to suppress the body's reaction, but this medication has multiple side effects.

Chronic bronchitis is an inflammation of the bronchial tubes, which leads to excessive mucus and thick secretions. This blocks the bronchi and interferes with breathing. A chronic productive cough lasting for three months in two consecutive years is diagnostic for chronic bronchitis. If infection is present, antibiotics may help. Medication can dilate the bronchi to increase airflow. Fluids are encouraged and a humidifier placed in the room, so that respiratory secretions are less dry and thick and can be coughed up.

Emphysema is an abnormal enlargement of the small air sacs in the lung, due to destruction of the air sac walls. Air pollutants encountered while working in certain occupations and smoking can predispose a person to develop emphysema. Clean air, no smoking, and bronchodilators will help. A person becomes so used to the high level of carbon dioxide in his blood when he has emphysema that it no longer acts as a stimulus for breathing. The low level of oxygen in his blood takes over as a stimulus for breathing. A person with emphysema who needs oxygen therapy has to be very careful that the oxygen is kept at a low concentration; otherwise the person will lose his stimulus to breathe.

It takes time for the signs and symptoms of COPD to develop: fatigue due to lack of oxygen, cough, and shortness of breath on exertion, barrel-shaped chest. The person with emphysema is taught how to breathe in a way that will keep the bronchi dilated, so that he can breathe out the carbon dioxide. An exercise program is necessary to prevent invalidism. Disuse of muscles makes them weaker. A nutritious diet may reverse the weight loss caused by lack of appetite and the increased energy demands of difficulty in breathing. The American Lung Association has a booklet, *Help Yourself to Better Breathing*, with tips for people with respiratory problems.

Pneumonia

In pneumonia, the lungs are inflamed and their secretions fill the small air sacs. This reduces the amount of oxygen absorbed from the air, so the tissues do not obtain the oxygen they need, and the person feels tired and weak—even after the fever (if present) goes down. If a person has a chronic cardiac or respiratory condition, penumonia may kill him.

It is necessary to encourage fluids to keep the secretions liquid, so that they can be coughed up and the air passages cleared. Antibiotics, rest, and oxygen will be prescribed.

Suggestions

1 Describe the signs and symptoms of lack of an adequate blood supply to the brain.
2 Enroll in a CPR class.
3 Investigate the following resources:
   Heart Disease: Heartlife (800)241-6993, (404)523-0626 in Georgia, answers questions on heart diseases and pacemakers and distributes a quarterly periodical entitled *Pulse*.
   Lung Diseases: Lungline (800)222-5864, (303)398-1477 in Colorado, answers questions about asthma, emphysema, allergies, chronic bronchitis, smoking and other respiratory and immune system disorders. Questions are answered by registered nurses or other health professionals. A service of the National Jewish Center for Immunology and Respiratory Medicine.

cancer

Cells have the potential to become malignant when they divide. A cancer cell somehow resists the body's command to stop and keeps multiplying and growing. Cancer is the leading cause of death after heart disease.

Normally the immune system protects the body by reacting to the stimulus of mutated cells, bacteria or viruses. The stimulus causes the body to make antibodies against the foreign substance. Other non-specific body defenses include gastric acid, which does not provide a good medium for bacterial growth; the increased motility of the intestine when foreign substances which irritate the intestine need to be eliminated; and intact mucous membranes and skin to prevent the entrance of bacteria into the body.

As the immune system becomes less efficient with aging, its capability to fight infection and destroy mutated malignant cells decreases. There is an increase in autoantibodies, which misinterpret a person's own cells as a foreign substance, and attack the person's own cells. A cancer cell which is not destroyed invades the local normal tissue, stealing its nutrients and through pressure cutting off its blood supply and causing pain. In addition to this action, the cancer cell can be carried by the blood to other parts of the body, to multiply and become what is known as a metastatic tumor (a secondary tumor from a primary tumor located elsewhere.)

There are many theories about what causes a cell to become malignant. One theory suggests that certain people have genes that are more inclined to develop cancer, given exposure to agents that cause cancer, such as, radiation, chemicals or viruses.

Warning Signs

The American Cancer Society suggests that we look out for the following major warning signs of cancer:

C—Change in bowel or bladder habits
A—A sore that does not heal
U—Unusual bleeding or discharge
T—Thickening or lump in breast or elsewhere
I—Indigestion or difficulty in swallowing
O—Obvious change in wart or mole
N—Nagging cough or hoarseness

The local signs and symptoms of a cancer depend upon where the tumor is located. It can exert pressure upon a nerve, causing pain, or exert pressure on a blood vessel cutting off the blood supply. A person can also show more general signs and symptoms, such as weight loss, fatigue, or infection.

Treatment

Since the cause of cancer is unknown, the treatment is not aimed at one specific cause, but attacks the cancer cells in different ways. If the entire tumor is removed by surgery, and the cancer has not spread (metastasized) to other parts of the body, then the person can be cured.

Any surgery carries the risk of infection, when the intact skin—a barrier to infection—is cut. This is a particular problem when an elderly person has cancer, since the metabolic demands of a tumor take nutrients away from other cells in the body. Also, the immune system is depressed and cannot fight infection effectively. Surgery interrupts the blood supply to surrounding tissue, so the more extensive the surgery, the more the chance of hemorrhage and shock for the patient.

A person who has to undergo surgery is worried and under stress, particularly when the surgery is for cancer, a diagnosis which most people perceive to be a death sentence. The surgery itself is traumatic to the body, which must adjust to blood loss and to the loss of whatever organ was removed. After surgery, it takes time for other organs to recover from the effects of the anesthetic.

Radiation therapy may be a treatment on its own, or it may be used after surgery to try to kill any cancer cells remaining after surgery.

Radiation side effects depend upon the site irradiated. For example, nausea, vomiting, diarrhea, or bladder inflammation may occur when the radiation injures the normal tissue as well as the cancer tissue.

A patient who needs the therapy of an applicator of radioactive material inserted into her vagina will be placed on bed rest. Pregnant women and children under eighteen years should not visit. Staff and visitors will be given instructions about the time allowed in the patient's room, and the distance from which you should talk to her. The patient will have a catheter and low residue diet to keep the bladder and bowel empty. After the correct dose has been delivered, then the doctor removes the applicator, in the patient's room. The patient can then gradually resume activities.

Chemotherapy, using a combination of drugs which kill cancer cells, may be ordered. These drugs attack rapidly multiplying cancer cells. One problem is their toxicity, since they kill rapidly multiplying normal cells in the bone marrow, skin, and hair. Infection is a major hazard because of the diminished effectiveness of the immune system, caused by the chemotherapy drugs or aggravated by them. For example, mouth infection often occurs, unless teeth are brushed with a soft toothbrush after every meal. Antibiotics are ordered and mouth rinses.

A different approach is to use agents to stimulate the body's immune system. The theory behind this is that a more active immune system will be able to recognize the cancer cells as being foreign to the body and kill them. Sometimes a combination of therapies—surgery plus radiotherapy or chemotherapy, or both—may be appropriate.

Many cancers can be cured, if diagnosed early enough. However, the person may have a difficult time, while undergoing therapy. Lack of appetite, nausea and vomiting from radiotherapy lead to poor nutrition. Medication to control the vomiting will help. Diarrhea or constipation will necessitate diet changes and medication. Bleeding and anemia may require blood transfusions.

Pain can usually be controlled by oral medication taken on a regular schedule. Many people who are in pain wait too long until the pain is severe and difficult to control, because they are afraid of drug addiction. Elderly people are better medicated by using small dosages of drugs as ordered by their physician on a regular schedule, than by taking large doses of medication for severe pain, since the large dosages are more likely to cause side effects.

The pain experience may be made even more difficult by anxiety and depression. In most instances, a person should be told when he has cancer. However, no one can tell when a person is going to die. One should always maintain hope. A hospice or home health program offers support to family caregivers.

In the early stages of cancer, the person goes through cycles of illness and apparent health. At times the side effects of the treatment are worse than the signs and symptoms of the disease. A lump in the breast or lung may show no other signs and symptoms, whereas radiation or chemotherapy can make a person feel nauseated or tired. Radical surgery can leave a person post-operatively with the loss of a breast or an organ, draining tubes inserted into the operative site, pain and exhaustion. After recovery from the treatment and surgery, the person starts to feel well again. If the cancer is incurable then the cycle begins again as more treatments or different treatments are tried.

When my husband was in intensive care, I hesitated to tell my three college student children. They were about to take midterm exams, and I did not want to frighten them when we were waiting for a final diagnosis. However, I did tell them their father was ill and they dropped everything and caught the next plane home.

"You helped us, now it's our turn to help you." "I didn't cry when I saw all those tubes and how sick Dad was. I knew crying would make Dad feel bad." My husband was overjoyed to see them. I am used to being the professional nurse telling other people how to cope, so it was difficult for me to admit that I was in a state of shock, and needed help from others. When a colleague called me up and asked how my vacation was going, I answered, "Fine," because I did not want to talk about my problems. After she asked me to entertain and interview someone from out of town, I said, "I can't do that. My husband is in intensive care on a respirator." I don't think she will ask me about my vacation again. Eventually, the diagnosis was made that there was no cancer present. This awful experience made my husband and me more willing to receive help and support, and brought our whole family closer together.

It is advisable for people to carry some kind of health insurance for catastrophic illness. Chemotherapy charges can run into thousands of dollars. The social worker at the hospital or cancer clinic can offer advice about how to pay these charges.

Unless radical surgery directly affects sexual intercourse, sex would not be contraindicated. Anxiety and fatigue may interfere with ability to have a satisfying sexual experience. Mastectomy or colostomy surgery may lead a person to question her sexuality, in view of her changed appearance. A continuing kind, loving relationship will rebuild her confidence and self-esteem. Depending upon the type of surgery, breast implant reconstruction is a possibility—sometimes right after the mastectomy. The American Cancer Society offers a wealth of information and counseling for the person with cancer and his family.

If you attend a church, your minister, priest, or rabbi has much experience in counseling families facing terminal illness or death. A very sad situation is where an elderly couple have led a good life, and are prepared for one of them dying before the other—then they lose a child. A retired friend drove out to California with his wife, to visit their only son—a brilliant M.I.T. graduate. They drove home with his ashes. Then they entered a long period of mourning, reminiscing about happy times when their son was young. Later the father joined his wife's church. He stated, "This church is not just socializing. It really has something to say to you, when you're in trouble."

Sites of Cancer

The most common sites of cancer are the skin, lungs, colon, rectum, prostate, stomach, and breast. Skin cancer is caused by over-exposure to the sun, so it can be seen and treatment is sought early. Fair skinned people are most at risk. The cancer is surgically removed.

A cancer of the bronchial tubes is related to smoking, asbestos, and other environmental hazards. In the elderly, this is a slow-growing tumor so the person may die of some other health problem before the cancer would kill him. The person may have a cough, chest pain, and coughing up blood. To confirm the diagnosis, the doctor will order a chest X-ray, examination of the bronchus by inserting a tube into it and obtaining a sample (biopsy) of the tumor, sputum examination, and surgery if necessary. Surgery is the treatment of choice. Lung cancer is the most frequent cancer killer of men, and the rate of lung cancer among women is threatening to overtake the rate of breast cancer.

Colon and rectal cancer may be mistaken for hemorrhoids when blood is noticed in the stool. There may also be changes in the bowel pattern or in the shape of the stool, diarrhea or constipation. If the cancer is extensive, part of the bowel is removed and a colostomy may be necessary. Surgical blood loss may be 2000 cc. A colostomy is an opening into the colon through the abdomen, to provide for bowel elimination when the rectum is closed in surgery.

People can wear a colostomy bag to catch the stool, or can control the bowel evacuation by irrigation. They are taught how to do this by a nurse. Diet is also important to prevent gas and diarrhea or constipation. Many older men have problems with prostate gland enlargement which obstructs urination. If the enlargement is caused by cancer, the surgical excision has to be more extensive. There may be post-operative problems related to bleeding, infection, impotence, or incontinence. Stool softeners help to prevent bleeding because of straining. Antibiotics will be prescribed for any infection. It may take time to regain bladder control. Impotence may be a problem if nerves affecting the sexual response have been severed. Sexual counseling will help.

Cancer of the stomach may evidence itself by nausea, vomiting, or blood in the stool. Surgery excising the whole tumor is necessary. Deep breathing and coughing after surgery helps to prevent respiratory complications. Bleeding may lead to shock, so the blood pressure is monitored carefully. There will be a nasogastric tube in place, to suction secretions and prevent vomiting until the intestines resume their rhythmic movement and recover from the anesthesia. At that time, intravenous therapy will gradually be replaced by oral feeding.

The dumping syndrome is a problem specific to gastric surgery. When only a small amount of stomach remains after surgery, food leaves the stomach too quickly. Soon after eating (ten to thirty minutes) the person feels faint and dizzy. One way to prevent this problem is to lie down after eating to delay stomach emptying. Fluids taken between meals are encouraged, while fluids taken with meals are limited to decrease fullness.

The cause of breast cancer is unknown. Unmarried women are at a greater risk than women who have had children before the age of twenty-seven. The cancer is usually a non-tender lump, found when performing a breast examination or taking a bath. Removal of a breast is associated with a loss of sexuality in many women's perceptions, although various breast forms look natural, even under a swimsuit. Sometimes the arm on the same side as the mastectomy retains fluid, because of tissue drainage problems as a result of the surgery. Elevation of the involved arm promotes drainage and prevents swelling of the arm.

Cancer of the cervix is curable in its early stages. It may be asymptomatic or it may be discovered when the person notes a blood-stained vaginal discharge. Radiation is commonly prescribed.

For prevention of both cancer of the cervix and cancer of the uterus, a simple, painless, annual Pap test detects premalignant cell changes and indicates the need for six-month check-ups. However, the Pap test does not discover all cancers in the uterus, so post-menopausal bleeding may be the warning sign. If a hysterectomy is indicated, then the person will have a nasogastric tube after surgery; she will probably wear elastic stockings to promote circulation, and may need iron supplements because of blood loss. Since the ureters and bladder may be damaged during surgery, a catheter is inserted, left in the bladder, and monitored for blood.

Suggestions

1 Write to the American Cancer Society and ask for information on how to prevent cancer.
2 Investigate the following resources:
Cancer: AMC Cancer Information (800)525-3777, provides current information on causes of cancer, prevention, methods of detection and diagnosis, treatment and treatment facilities, rehabilitation, and counseling services. A service of AMC Cancer Research Center, Denver, Colorado.
Cancer Information Service (CIS): (800)4-CANCER, (800) 638-6070 in Arkansas, (808)524-1234 in Oahu, Hawaii (Neighbor Islands call collect), answers cancer-related questions from the public, cancer patients and families, and health professionals. The CIS staff members do not diagnose cancer or recommend treatment for individual cases. Spanish-speaking staff members are available to callers from the following areas: California, Florida, Georgia, Illinois, northern New Jersey, New York City, and Texas. A service of the National Cancer Institute.

common chronic health problems

As family members age, there are often multiple health problems in the family. I asked Pearl Lundquist to share with me what are some of the problems she encounters in her work with the Grant County Visiting Neighbor Program in Strandburg, South Dakota. Here are some specific examples of program recipients:

(1) Farm family of three:

> Mother—45—Diabetic. Double leg amputee, losing eyesight rapidly, in wheelchair.
>
> Father—Farmer—healthy—ambitious—honest.
>
> Son—11—healthy—very helpful to both parents.

Financial conditions poor, due to extensive medical bills. Program provides assistance six to eight hours weekly (laundry, cleaning, personal care). With this assistance the family remains intact, they are very appreciative. Relatives, friends, church contribute some to program on behalf of this family.

(2) Husband—96—Stroke—Just recently entered nursing home. Has participated in program for 12 years. After recent hospitalization he received daily care for a time.

> Wife—93—Heart plus other. Is able to live by herself with weekly assists.

Both have been in rather poor health for all 12 years, and have truly appreciated personal care and household assistance. They have always contributed small amounts which are added to the budgeted monies.

(3) Wife—multiple sclerosis—needs personal care daily—unable to move about on own (late 60s).

Husband—lung and back problems—(late 60s).
Contribute nearly full cost of care we provide. Would be in nursing home without this care.

(4) Mother—32—Lymph glands and voice box removed (cancer).
Husband—quarry worker.
Children—three: ages 12, 4, and 11 months. Elderly grandmother requested assistance as she helps care for children.
Mother unable to lift, vacuum, etc. The family is able to stay together with part-time assistance.

(5) Elderly—general health problems we alleviate by part-time help.
Heart, Alzheimer's disease, arthritis, physical personal care following hospitalization (particularly since new Medicare policy restricts hospital stays). Stroke requires long-term care. Terminal patients receive care as needed.

Many clients improve and may go off and on program as need allows. Service can be restored quickly if discontinued, which results in financial savings. Flexibility advantages. Several hundred clients have never had to be institutionalized as a result of this assistance. Children living out of the area feel secure about parents with this care available.

(6) Muscular dystrophy—Two grown sons being cared for by elderly mother—she developed blood pressure problems. Aide assisted daily with personal care (bath, getting them dressed) until time when one son passed away. Second son was served for several more years but was placed eventually in a nursing home. Both have passed away now. Mother's health was spared due to this help.

(7) With household assistance quite a number of retarded persons can live by themselves.

Recurring Fractures

A simple fracture is a break in the bone, without breaking the skin. A compound fracture is a break in the bone, where the skin is broken also. The signs and symptoms of a fracture are: pain, loss of function, swelling and discoloration of the skin. Emergency treatment consists of immobilizing the fracture in its current position, without attempting to straighten the bone, and calling an emergency service for help.

With a simple fracture, the doctor pulls the bones until they are in their normal position. A cast helps maintain the normal position until the bone heals. Skeletal traction pulls the bones into normal position and maintains that position, until the bone heals. The elderly take a longer time to heal, and are at risk for the hazards of immobility. Therefore, usually the doctor will go ahead with surgery and insert a metal plate and screws to protect the break until it heals.

Elderly women are at risk of a hip fracture because of osteoporosis. Hemorrhage and shock are immediate potential problems. An embolism of fat or bone marrow can lodge in the respiratory system or central nervous system and cause death. An embolism detached from a blood clot has the same result. All open wounds of a compound fracture are considered to be contaminated.

Delayed union means that the fracture has not healed in the average time for this type of fracture. Nonunion means that union is not expected to occur. Necrosis of bone means that the bone loses its blood supply. A person with a fracture needs to have circulation, movement, and sensation checked every two hours, because impaired circulation leads to tissue death and gangrene. The check is made below the level of the cast or traction.

Arthritis

Osteoarthritis is a degenerative joint disease, caused by wear on the joints. Elderly obese people develop pain and stiffness on the weight-bearing joints. Weight loss and an occupation that does not demand a lot of standing will help. Aspirin controls the pain.

Joint replacement is done for pain relief. After surgery, the person may have respiratory problems if he doesn't turn and cough and deep breathe, to prevent excessive build-up of respiratory secretions in the lungs. He may also develop problems with cardiovascular stress, hemorrhage, gastrointestinal ulcer, and phlebitis—inflammation of a blood vessel—which can lead to a pulmonary embolism. The prosthesis—artificial replacement of the joint—needs to "bond" to the patient's bone. If the prosthesis becomes infected, then the prosthesis will need to be removed. If all goes well, the person can be independent twenty-one days after surgery.

Rheumatoid arthritis is different from osteoarthritis, because the rheumatoid form is a systemic disease, not a local disease. Early signs include: fatigue, muscle stiffness, joint pain, and sometimes fever. Then the joints become swollen and lose their motion. Treatment includes: rest, physical therapy, drugs to control pain and inflammation, surgery. If joints are painful and swollen, it is necessary to rest them. Later a gradual exercise program is introduced. Aspirin controls the pain and inflammation. Other drugs, such as steroids, may need to be added to the regime as the disease progresses. It has not been proved that any special diet will prevent arthritis.

A person with arthritis should sit down while working. Joints may need splints to rest joints and prevent deformity. All kitchen storage areas should be within reach. There are various long-handled assistive devices on the market.

Mealtime Manual (for people with disabilities and the aging) is prepared by the Institute of Rehabilitation Medicine, New York University Medical Center and Campbell Soup Company. The book has many helpful hints about cooking with a disability, including protective techniques to help people with arthritis:

- Use large joints instead of small ones.
- Avoid tasks requiring great manual strength.
- Avoid prolonged holding as much as possible.
- Begin an activity only if you can call a halt to it.
- Select lightweight utensils
- Find new ways to transport items.
- Let others share in the jobs by doing the lifting and carrying of heavy items.

For more information about arthritis, write to the Arthritis Foundation, 3400 Peachtree Road, N.E., Atlanta, Georgia 30326.

Diabetes

In diabetes, a deficiency in insulin leads to impaired carbohydrate metabolism, and an elevated blood sugar. Several factors are implicated in the problem of a deficiency in insulin: damage to the cells in the pancreas which secrete insulin, lessened activity of the insulin which is present, and a need for additional insulin because of stress, obesity, infection, and other conditions which increase metabolism.

Type I diabetes is insulin-dependent and is associated with a viral infection, a heredity trait in the genes, lack of insulin, and juvenile onset. Type II diabetes includes non-insulin-dependent diabetes, associated with secretion of insufficient insulin to metabolize carbohydrates, and adult onset diabetes. Insulin is given by subcutaneous injection to Type I diabetics. There is no oral insulin, because it would be broken down in the stomach, before it had a chance to work. Other oral medication, which stimulates the pancreas to secrete more insulin, may be given.

Elderly obese people are at risk for diabetes, since the secretion of insulin decreases with age and is not enough to meet the person's need for insulin as he puts on weight. Today, more people are aware of the signs and symptoms of diabetes, and they are going to the doctor for help with this problem. The main symptoms are: an increase of urine, because the kidney is trying to excrete more sugar in the urine to bring the high level of blood sugar to normal; thirst, because of the increased urination; hunger and weight loss, because fat and protein are being broken down for energy in the place of carbohydrates, which need insulin to be absorbed effectively.

Adult onset diabetics are less likely to go into acidosis from too little insulin, or hypoglycemia from too much insulin. However, the oral drugs given to stimulate insulin secretion can also have side effects. Diabetics can have problems with atherosclerosis, impaired kidney function, blindness, infection, and foot problems. If a diabetic cuts his foot while attempting to remove a corn, the cut may become infected and also gangrene—tissue death—is a possibility. Amputation may be necessary, because gangrene becomes infected and will not heal. Avoiding injury to the feet is essential—toenails should be cut straight across; no harsh solutions on the feet; a podiatrist should remove corns.

Diet, exercise, and drugs are major tools for control of diabetes. The American Diabetic Association has a booklet called the *Exchange Lists for Meal Planning*. After a dietitian has counseled the client, the exchange method of meal planning is simple. The six major exchange lists are:

List	1	Milk exchanges	Milk
	2	Vegetable exchanges	All Non-Starchy Vegetables
	3	Fruit exchanges	All Fruits and Fruit Juices
	4	Bread exchanges	Bread, Cereal, Pasta, Starchy Vegetables
	5	Meat exchanges	Lean Meat, Medium-Fat Meat, High-Fat Meat
	6	Fat exchanges	Polyunsaturated, Saturated

The doctor prescribes the number of calories and type of diet desired. The dietitian teaches the patient how to use the exchange lists. A diabetic taking insulin may start to put on weight, because the glucose is now stored, instead of being excreted in the urine. An exercise regimen will help avoid this weight gain.

Urine testing for glucose is done to ascertain if the insulin dosage is enough to prevent glucose being wasted in the urine, instead of being used by the body. Blood sugar monitoring can now be done at home with a blood sample taken in a finger stick. If they are outside the limits defined as normal, then contact a doctor.

The doctor should also explain to the diabetic how to cope with periods of illness. A diabetic usually controlled by oral drugs may have to be given insulin during post-surgical care, when he is taking nothing by mouth. If the health problem involves a one-day bout with nausea and vomiting, then the person can follow the sick day regimen, already prescribed by the doctor, and call him as necessary.

Gastrointestinal Problems

Dennis Hyams, M.D., shared with me information about the causes and symptoms of gastrointestinal problems in the old. Abdominal pain may be present with no other physical signs. Diverticulitis is a condition where small sacs form in the colon. Pieces of stool are trapped in these sacs and the colon becomes inflamed. There may be no symptoms of this inflammation, or the person may exhibit fever, pain, tenderness, and rectal bleeding. To prevent diverticulitis, increasing the amount of bran in the diet ensures more frequent bowel movements, and apparently diminishes the amount of stool trapped in the colon sacs. Once infection is present, antibiotics, stool softeners, pain drugs, and even surgery may be required.

Jaundice is usually caused by gallstones, a side effect of drugs, or obstruction by a tumor. For selected patients, gallstones may be dissolved by oral medications. Research is continuing in this area to prevent the need for surgery. Women are more likely to develop gallbladder infection. If weight reduction, antibiotics, and fat restriction do not solve the problem, then surgery may be necessary.

Cirrhosis of the liver is a result of destruction of the liver cells, which diminishes the ability of the liver to carry out its functions of metabolizing carbohydrates and detoxification of drugs. Cirrhosis may be the result of alcohol abuse, medication side effects, or a chemical insult. The outcome depends upon how severe the liver damage is. The treatment is to remove the cause—alcohol, medication, or chemical—to give the liver a chance to recover. The liver may lose around eighty percent of its functioning cells before liver failure and death are inevitable.

Nausea and vomiting may result from gastrointestinal problems, heart failure, and other diseases. Treat the cause. If it is not possible to eliminate the cause of the nausea and vomiting, then medication to relieve the problem can be given.

Urinary Tract Problems

Urinary tract infections can be caused by an ascent of germs from the anal area. Women have a shorter tube leading into the bladder and may have infections following sexual intercourse. Infection is more common in women than men. In the lower urinary tract, infection may manifest itself by pain and frequency in urination. In the urinary tract above the bladder, pain over the kidney area and pain on urination will be present. Antibiotics and encouraging fluids helps.

Kidney failure as a result of slow decline in function leads to retention of sodium, water, and the end products of protein metabolism. A build-up of these products of protein waste brings neurological complications—drowsiness leading to coma and death. Other problems are present: anemia, nausea and vomiting and metabolic acidosis.

The conservative management of kidney failure focuses on replacement of fluid and electrolyte losses to maintain a level within normal limits. The amount of protein in the diet is restricted, to limit protein waste. This means that the protein taken must be of top quality to meet the body's needs, since the person will not be eating a large variety of foods.

Kidney dialysis is a means of clearing waste products, when the kidney ceases functioning. A tube is inserted into the abdominal cavity. A specially prepared fluid is run in. Time is allowed for waste products and substances at a higher than normal level in the blood to filter into this special fluid. Then, the fluid is drained out of the abdominal cavity through the tube. The schedule for how often this has to be done is ordered by the doctor.

Another method for clearing the wastes is to insert a tube into the blood circulation. Blood is circulated through a machine with special fluid, which replenishes lost electrolytes, reduces the blood potassium level if necessary, and clears waste products. Tubing, called a shunt, is left in place to provide access to the blood circulation, without sticking the patient with a large needle every time the dialysis has to be done. Possible complications of this method are hemorrhage and infection.

In Chapter 15, cancer of the prostate was discussed. A more common prostate problem is benign prostate hypertrophy. This is an enlargement associated with an increase in the size and numbers of the cells. The reason for this is thought to be a hormonal imbalance as men age. Early signs of this problem are: urinary frequency accompanied by awakening to void at night, a smaller urinary stream, and difficulty in voiding. When the bladder is not completely emptied, then the urine left in the bladder is more likely to grow bacteria, and the bladder is more likely to contain stones. Also, if the bladder is not emptied, pressure builds up in the kidneys and eventually the pressure will ruin kidney function.

Medical treatment for enlargement of the prostate gland consists of antibiotics if an infection is present, and measures to expel excess secretions, such as massage and sexual intercourse. Surgical treatment consists of introducing a tube into the bladder and cutting away the part of the prostate that is pressing on the urethra and preventing urination. Because of the danger of hemorrhage, a catheter with an inflatable 25 cc balloon is left in place, to exert pressure on the area from which the gland was taken. Also, a continuous system of bladder irrigation is set up, to prevent blood clots interfering with catheter drainage, since the bladder has a rich blood supply. There may be dribbling of urine, until the muscles regain their strength after the stress of surgery. A radical excision of tissue for cancer may cause nerve damage and impotence.

Suggestions

1 List the signs and symptoms of hyperglycemia and hypoglycemia in a diabetic.
2 Investigate the following resources:
   Diabetes: American Diabetes Association, (800)232-3472, (703) 549-1500 in Virginia, provides free printed materials, newsletter, and health education information and gives physician referrals and support group assistance information.
   Kidney Disease: American Kidney Fund (800)638-8299, (800) 492-8361 in Maryland, grants financial assistance to kidney patients who are unable to pay treatment costs. Also provides information on organ donations and kidney-related diseases.

loss of intellect

The symptoms of loss of intellect include forgetfulness and confusion. While people used to dismiss these symptoms as incurable effects of old age, they are not necessarily so. Five percent of Americans over sixty-five years suffer from a permanent, irreversible, severe loss of intellect. Another ten percent have mild loss of intellect.

Acute Organic Brain Syndrome

Sometimes an injury to the brain tissue can mimic Alzheimer's disease. The side effects of drugs can cause confusion. Poor nutrition can cause fluid and electrolyte imbalances, which damage the brain tissue. A vitamin B_1 deficiency is prevalent in alcoholics, due to their inadequate diet. This deficiency may impair the memory for recent events. Cardiac and lung problems interfere with sufficient oxygen reaching the brain.

If the cause can be treated, then the temporary reversible confusion will get better. Drugs can be stopped or their dosage reduced. Nutrition teaching prevents deficiencies. Alcoholics Anonymous is a resource organization for alcohol abusers. Seeking help is the first step towards sobriety and a better life. If the cardiac and lung problems can be alleviated, then the damage to the brain tissue may be reversible. It is essential for the doctor to differentiate between the acute organic brain syndrome and a chronic organic brain syndrome, instead of accepting confusion as a normal part of aging.

Emotional problems can be mistaken for organic brain syndrome.

Depression can make a person slow and confused. Loss of self-esteem, loneliness, anxiety, and boredom can become more common as elderly persons face retirement and the deaths of relatives and friends. Antidepressant medication and counseling may help. A balanced diet, exercise, and involvement in social activities also help in avoiding depression.

Alzheimer's Disease

A loss of intellect affecting men and women between forty and sixty years, characterized by progressive, irreversible deterioration of the intellect is referred to as Alzheimer's disease. This is thought to be the same disease process as chronic organic brain syndrome, occurring at an earlier age. There is a decrease of brain cells. Also, the brain tissue shows plaques and a twisting of nerve fibers, called tangles. On occasion, chronic organic brain syndrome is caused by multiple small strokes, associated with poor cerebrovascular circulation and brain tissue death, but this cause is unusual.

Another name for Alzheimer's disease and chronic organic brain syndrome is dementia. The National Institutes of Health has a booklet, *The Dementias: Hope Through Research*, which provides information about loss of intellect. Various factors have been suggested to influence the occurrence of Alzheimer's disease. Neurotransmitters in the brain carry messages. A deficiency in this area may be implicated. Excessively large amounts of aluminum have been found in the nerve tangles, but the relationship of this to Alzheimer's disease is unknown. There may be a genetic component or autoimmune component in the development of this disease.

Very little research is being done on people with organic brain syndrome, since they are unable to give consent to become participants in a study. It is essential that these people receive protection from being experimented on. However, a lack of *in vivo* investigations with humans may be one reason that it has been so difficult to find a cure for organic brain syndrome. The National Institutes of Health sponsors research banks, which accept postmortem brain tissue donated by families after their elderly relative dies. These banks are trying to determine what causes organic brain syndrome.

Research is being conducted to determine if diet or drug therapy will improve the action of neurotransmitters. Drugs to eliminate aluminum from the body are being given, since there is excess aluminum in the brain tangles of people with Alzheimer's disease. Another possibility is that a viral disease attacks the brain cells and alters the genes, so that they cannot reproduce normally, but form the tangles.

The spouse of a person with dementia may himself be elderly and very worried about what will happen to his wife when he is no longer able to serve as a caregiver. It may be possible to slow down the rate of decline by stimulating the person and encouraging as much independence as possible. Orient the person to time, place, and person. Provide a very large calendar, list of daily activities, and written notes about safety measures; label commonly used items. For advice contact: Alzheimer's Disease and Related Disorders Association, 360 North Michigan Avenue, Chicago, Illinois 60601.

Rehabilitation

The Burke Rehabilitation Center in New York sent me information about their Senior Day Care Program for patients with dementia. It provides respite for caretakers, a safe and therapeutic environment, and an effective alternative to institutionalization. In the Burke Program, each individual is assessed by physicians to determine the extent and nature of the loss of intellect. Then the diagnosis and treatment plan are discussed by the family.

The program is conducted four days a week. Primary areas of activity are memory training and reminiscence, physical activity, social interaction, and family support. Memory training aids are: a posted daily schedule, photographs of staff and patients, and large clocks and calendars, along with frequent orientation to date, time, place, and person. Reminiscence is stimulated by the use of the creative arts therapies: art, music, and dance therapy.

The program runs from 9:15 a.m. to 3:30 p.m. The schedule involves:

- reception
- reality orientation
- memory training and reminiscence
- movement therapy/exercise
- lunch

The variable afternoon schedule includes two or more of: art therapy, dance therapy, current events, group psychotherapy, music therapy, and games.

Upon entering the program, twelve patients showed a three-month temporary period of slightly improved cognitive and physical function.

Repeated evaluation showed a steady decline in functional abilities, when followed up for eighteen months. This is a very small sample. But it certainly does not indicate that day care halts the downward decline and death of people with dementia. However, the day care did assist patients and families to adapt to the decline. Families received a much-needed respite period.

One family member stated, "The release from care for a few hours brings renewed strength to handle the remainder of the day." In addition, families believed that the knowledge obtained from staff allowed them to take an active role in preventing institutionalization. The Burke program is covered by Medicaid. A sliding scale fee is available for those without adequate insurance coverage. Families perceived that without day care, they would have been forced to place the person in a nursing home or hire additional help at home.

Abuse of the Aged

A potential problem when elderly people have severe physical and mental problems is elder abuse. The abusers are usually relatives who are under a lot of stress and use alcohol or drugs. They have difficulty in meeting the needs of an elderly person who requires a lot of care, but usually they perceive that they cannot give up the money that they receive from the elderly person by keeping her in their home.

There is a personality problem involved in this situation. The abuser may have been the victim of child abuse. Ultimately, we just do not know why some caregivers become abusive. Professional counseling may help in this situation. Unless the person is receiving physical abuse, it is probably preferable to try to maintain her in her family situation and offer support to the whole family in solving this problem.

Suggestions

1 What are the signs and symptoms of acute organic brain syndrome?

2 How could you manage the care of a person with Alzheimer's Disease?

3 Alzheimer's Disease: Alzheimer's Disease and Related Disorders Association (800)621-0379, (800)572-6037 in Illinois. Obtain information on publications about Alzheimer's disease and related disorders available from the Association. If needed, obtain referral to local chapters and support groups.

elderly volunteers

The middle-aged housewife who used to perform needed volunteer work is now often involved in a full-time job. Elders become bored, sitting home watching TV. The healthy elderly can find fulfillment by helping people of all ages and backgrounds.

Helping People in Detention

Linnette Pryor described the Grandparent Pen Pal program in Arkansas, which involves volunteers in the criminal justice program:

> We made our first contact with the prison chaplain. Our chaplain surveyed prisoners that were not receiving correspondence or visitation of any kind and asked them if they would like to have a pen pal. The chaplain then turned in the names to me.
>
> After putting together this list, I began surveying volunteers. After the volunteers applied for the program they were trained according to the regulations for the Arkansas Department of Corrections. Information was given to them concerning prison rules, what to inform the prison of, if they were to receive a letter telling them of an escape or suicide attempt, and even what to talk about in their letters.
>
> After the training, volunteer references were checked. We wanted to make sure we had volunteers that would be a good influence on the prisoner. When I received all the reference information, I wrote a letter to each volunteer and gave them the name of their new pen pal.
>
> The volunteers were instructed to write the prisoner, signing the letter with only their first name. They were told to return the letter to my office in the return envelope I had enclosed for them to use. After the letter arrived at my office, I removed it from the original envelope and placed it

in a plain white envelope and addressed it to the prisoner. The return address on the envelope only included the first name of the volunteer, my post office box, city, state and zip code. For example:

Ruby
P.O. Box 5035
Jonesboro, AR 72403

The volunteers for our program do not live in Jonesboro, so there is no way for a possibly unscrupulous inmate to harm the volunteer, once they leave prison. When the inmates write a return letter, I receive it and put it in an envelope addressed to the volunteer complete with a preaddressed return envelope.

Many of our volunteers are homebound and the inmate's letter is the only mail they receive. Several of the inmates do not read or write. They mention in their letters that they have someone read their mail to them and write their return letters. Some inmates say they enjoy the letters so much they have friends read the letter to them over and over again.

Often when the pen pals send their letters to me to be forwarded, they also write me a note. Some quotes from those notes are as follows:

"Thank you for helping me find a new friend."

"I am home bound and don't see many people or get much mail. I go to the mail box every day to see if my pen pal wrote me."

"My letter from C. J. was sad, but informative. I keep all my letters they are special."

"I was so happy to get my first letter. He wrote a nice one and yes he needs friends too."

From an out of state man in the Arkansas prison system came the following:

"I am from another state and was so surprised when a stranger from Arkansas cared enough to write, my family doesn't even do that."

Our program is designed with the intention of reducing the feelings of violence and abandonment the inmate feels toward the society that placed him in prison. Our pen pals encourage the inmates and show them they have a genuine interest in their progress. Statistics show the individual contact can reduce the recidivism rate.

For further information call Linnette Pryor at the East Arkansas Area Agency on Aging.

Every Tuesday a group of seniors board a bus in Rossmoor, California. They are the Senior Tutors en route to the Youth Guidance Center in San Francisco, to tutor teenage boys and girls who have been committed by the Juvenile Court for periods ranging from 30 to 90 days. Each tutor will spend two hours from 1:00 p.m. to 3:00 p.m. with an assigned teenager. Together they work on class assignments, do crafts projects, play games, or just talk.

These intergenerational relationships were initiated to offer the youth opportunities to grow in self-esteem, develop new insights, and make plans for a better life. The Senior Tutors are warm, patient, and concerned adult friends. The teenagers are helped with their homework when help is requested and needed. Many suffer from learning disabilities. The tutors bring in personally chosen educational materials and every effort is made to stimulate and interest them in continuing their educations. Each achievement is praised—those who experience difficulties are encouraged to persevere.

When the teenagers desire to talk about their problems such as drugs, or the temptations of their peer group, they are encouraged to examine their own individual responsibilities. The tutors have a wealth of life experiences to call on and they use them in creative ways. Thought-provoking stories and articles are offered to create new life goals and stimulate self-examination. One youth's statement, "I don't ever want to come back here again," can be an opener for counselling opportunities. Rewards for the tutors? "It is in a sense a religious experience to touch this clouded young life with a momentary radiance." For more information contact Senior Tutors For Youth in Detention, 484-40 Lake Park Avenue, Oakland, California, 94610.

Intergenerational Projects

Linda Lee Davis, Director, furnished details about the San Antonio Foster Grandparent Program. She stated,

> I learn something from these wonderful people every day. I am a better person from having the opportunity to be a part of their lives.
>
> The Foster Grandparent Program does the impossible. It pleases everybody! It pleases the grandparents, both financially and psychologically; it pleases host institutions by allowing better care for their children; and it pleases the public, whose tax dollars and private donations turn into a sound financial investment with a high rate of return.
>
> The purpose of the Foster Grandparent Program is to provide the opportunity for low-income people aged 60 and older to contribute usefully to their community at no cost to themselves. The Grandparents receive a $2.20 stipend per hour for their four hour a day, five day a week service. Jesus Guerrero, eighty-five, states, "Without the Foster Grandparent Program, it would hurt my budget and I would be at home going to waste." The Grandparents receive transportation reimbursement, a hot meal, an annual physical examination, uniforms, and insurance at no cost.

At the Holmgreen Memorial Children's Shelter, forty percent of the children are taken to the Shelter by the police due to family crises, such as economic trouble, abuse/neglect, abandonment, incarceration or hospitalization of parents. The grandparents work one-to-one there with children needing special attention. This attention may range from dressing and feeding to socializing, helping with homework and most importantly, giving love to a frightened child.

"Two of the Children's Hospitals in San Antonio have foster grandparents working with the Play Therapist and assisting in the different medical units. The grandparents alleviate some of the concern parents have when they are not able to be with their child during the day, due to their own work, or because they live in another city and the child has been flown to San Antonio for treatment.

Foster grandparents assist with mentally retarded children's activities of daily living and in the school classrooms on a one-to-one basis at Mission Road Development Center. The grandparents also provide in-home substitute care to children who are active protective services clients.

More than half of all serious crimes in the U.S. are committed by youths aged 10–17. Since 1960, juvenile crime has risen twice as fast as that of adults. It is the intention of the Juvenile Court to help the youngster remain in the community, thereby giving him hope. He is also kept at the Juvenile Detention Center in order to keep him separated from adult criminals who can so easily influence young minds. It is hoped that foster grandparents giving themselves to these misguided youngsters will be able to influence them, to listen, to love, and to rehabilitate.

The Program has joined Project Any Baby Can in a home placement project in homes of medically involved infants, families with multiple handicaps, and poor prognosis. The grandparents provide support, assistance, and love to the family.

Foster grandparents are required to have four hours of inservice training a month to provide them with expanded knowledge about assignment related activities, supportive services available to them in the community and subjects of special interest. The questionnaire is a way to identify needed inservice. The combination of the annual physical, which has uncovered unknown illnesses, a warm meal each day of volunteering, transportation reimbursement, continued educational training, and the small stipend, used mostly for paying medical bills and for medicine, assists seniors to live independently as active productive community volunteers.

Uptown Center Hull House in Chicago has a program for latchkey children and grandparents called, "Grandma, Please!" According to Darcy Ehrman, Program Director,

This is a telephone helpline that links latchkey children with older adults and satisfies an ageless need for warm, human contact.

This is a way to meet the needs of mobility-limited and mobile older adults and latchkey children. The adults make a meaningful contribution to their community by praising, comforting, and reassuring the children that "someone is there to listen." Calls from the children reveal:

"Grandma, my parents are divorced . . ."
"Grandma, I got 100 on the test"
"You sound like Santa Claus, Grandpa."
"Grandma, we just won the baseball game, four to nothing!"
"Thanks for cheering me up."
"I love you Grandma!"

The Grandmas say, "These kids are doing more for me, than I am doing for them."

For further information, write to Ms. Ehrman at 4520 N. Beacon Street, Chicago, Illinois 60640.

John Murray, Director, furnished information on the "Helping Kids" program of the Senior Adult Education Program of Monroe, Michigan.

VOLUNTEER REGISTRATION FORM
TEACHING-LEARNING COMMUNITIES
ANN ARBOR PUBLIC SCHOOLS

(The first part of this form consists of basic data, name, etc.)

Availability to volunteer _____   Morning _____   Afternoon _____   M T W T F

Do you drive? _____   Do you need transportation provided? _____

Any physical limitations? _____   Languages spoken _____   Education level _____

Work Experience:

What would you like to do as a volunteer grandperson?

_____ crafts	_____ needlepoint	_____ dramatics
_____ woodworking	_____ embroidery	_____ story telling
_____ sewing	_____ cooking	_____ astronomy
_____ art	_____ electronics	_____ weaving
_____ music	_____ creative writing	_____ ceramics
_____ dance	_____ poetry	_____ science
_____ gardening	_____ photography	_____ other
_____ crocheting	_____ lace making	

What would you most enjoy doing with children and young people? _____

_____

Other skills and interests _____

How did you become interested in Teaching-Learning Communities? _____

_____   _____
Doctor's name   Person to call in emergency

A retired school administrator, James Steed, teaches a class, "Tutoring Skills," which prepares senior citizens to tutor children in the elementary school. The volunteers meet with Mr. Steed for about forty-five minutes each Friday morning. They discuss chapters in their textbook and exchange ideas on how to help children learn.

Then each senior spends half an hour with each of three students, doing work that the classroom teachers have suggested. The tutors function as teacher aides carrying out drills recommended by the teacher. The tutors make written comments about the child's work, and every six weeks the classroom teachers review the progress of each child. If he has accomplished the goals set for him, perhaps he will be replaced by some other student in the tutoring program for the next period. A sample application form is on preceeding page.

Suggestion

1 Find out the volunteer opportunities in your community, appropriate for elderly volunteers.

obtaining assistance from others

Thirty years ago it would be a rare phenomenon to see a frail, sick, abandoned old person straying around the Mayagüez plaza in Puerto Rico, but due to the loosening of family ties in modern society this became a common sight. The elderly were living as beggars, living in an inhuman condition—even searching for food in garbage cans. The typical beggar was a man aged sixty-seven, living alone with no family ties. He received his income from Social Services Department and was illiterate.

Father Gerardo, Mrs. Venegas of the Area Agency on Aging, and Mrs. Nieva, Director of La Milagrosa Day Care Center, joined together to help these people. An immediate priority was nutrition and education. Now the participants are no longer vagrants, but independent well-cared-for people. They read and proudly sign their names on a notebook, something they had never done before. "These people deserve to live as the human beings they are and to be loved and cared for."

This is an example of the work being done by the Area Agencies on Aging, to promote independence in the elderly. They are also willing to offer advice on local resources available for individual families. You will find the telephone number of your local Administration on Aging listed under the U.S. Government, Department of Health and Human Services, Office of Human Development Services. This Administration also publishes a journal, *Aging*. It is not an academic theoretical journal, but a practical handbook on aging, reporting on new developments and describing how various people and agencies have been successful in their projects to help the elderly.

173

Home Health Agencies

Visiting Nurse agencies were funded by corporations or foundations, and were nonprofit. Now that Medicare and Medicaid are paying for certain nursing services in the home, for-profit organizations have entered this field of health care. A friend told me that she recently paid $25 an hour for a home health nurse. The organization charged $25 and gave the nurse $10. This markup seems to be higher than it should be, although I can understand that the organization has management costs.

The university I work for has a nurse-managed clinic which does not charge clients for home visits. It receives money from grants and from the university. The amount of money obtainable limits the service to our local community. There is also a problem with time, since university faculty are expected to teach, do research, and publish. We are trying to develop a new model for service in the clinic, and I hope to become an active participant in this clinic next year.

As hospital beds remain unfilled, administrators consider designating certain units as extended care beds, and opening home health agencies. Mary Jane Koren, M.D., is Assistant Professor of Medicine at Montefiore Medical Center. She characterized their home health agency:

> Our first program is what is called a certified home health agency. This program provides skilled services to homebound patients who have a potential for recovery, recuperation, or rehabilitation. Patients therefore remain on it for a finite period of time. Depending on the problem this can be anywhere from a few days up to several months. By receiving visits from nurses, physical therapists, occupational therapists, speech therapists or medical social workers, the patient is returned either to his former level of functioning or to the highest level of functioning which can be achieved.
>
> The program is primarily funded at this time by Medicare, although in New York State Medicaid will also fund patients on this program. Many other third party payers also provide home care benefits. This program will become of increasing importance as Medicare payment regulations force the elderly patient out of the hospital, by mandating shorter lengths of stay.
>
> The availability in the home of intravenous therapy, ventilators, and other similar devices permits treatment at home to be both sophisticated and intensive. Medicare also funds a certain number of hours per day of home health aides, which can help the functionally disabled older person with acts of daily living and other light housekeeping or personal care chores. These services are not only available to patients from hos-

pitals, but are also accessible to patients in the community, either by their own self referral or through a doctor's referral. We have found that often by putting an out-patient on home care, we are able actually to avoid the necessity of a hospitalization, because the deteriorating physical condition can be reversed by providing nursing or therapy into the home.

The second program which we run is the Long-Term Home Health Care Program, which is also known as the Nursing Home Without Walls. This program was begun as a demonstration project in New York State, to see whether or not patients, who would otherwise be institutionalized could be kept in their own homes for a fraction of the cost that nursing home placement would necessitate. This program was conceived very much as an institutional replacement model. By this I mean that number of the available slots that any given agency could have was based on a statewide nursing home beds methodology (for example, for every 100,000 population you needed x number of nursing home beds and for every x number of nursing home beds you needed x number of Long-Term Home Health Care "beds"). Any program which wishes to expand beyond the allocated number of slots has to apply to the state for a certificate of need, just as they would have had to do were they trying to build more nursing home beds. Patients on this program also are rated on New York State's assessment instrument, used to determine level of institutional care needed. This tool rates people along cognitive and functional parameters and a number is assigned, which then permits them to bill Medicaid for either a health related facility (HRF) or skilled nursing facility (SNF) level care. All patients who are going to be brought on to the Long-Term Home Health Care Program must be rated on this scale and score in a range which would have otherwise qualified them for placement in a facility. Just as for nursing home placement Medicaid eligibility or the ability to pay out of pocket is required so they must "spend down" to a Medicaid level or be able to cover the cost themselves.

The amount of money which is allocated to this program is seventy-five percent of what it would cost to keep any individual at a comparable level of nursing home care. The current dollar amount for this is about $1300 per month for a patient at an HRF level, and $2300 per month for a patient at a SNF level. This can be annualized so some monthly flexibility exists. Since this program is felt to be a replacement for a nursing home, it provides chronic maintenance care with no time limits.

There is no need for them to improve or to meet any treatment goals. Our experience to date with this program is that it can in fact delay or forestall institutionalization in the elderly. However, as patients become more and more cognitively impaired or become less and less able to perform their own physical care needs, a strong informal support network is needed to keep the more severely impaired at home.

• • •

Senior Centers

Promoting independence in the elderly is often a group effort. They have unmet needs in physical and psychosocial areas, so their need for help will vary from time to time. A senior center provides a full range of social services, for people who do not require hospitalization. The services offered depend upon the location of the center and the nature of its population.

Tucker County Senior Citizens is located in one of the most isolated and mountainous areas of West Virginia. Per capita income is $5,102 annually. There is no public means of transportation other than the senior center van. There is one local weekly newspaper, no radio or television. Most of the county is owned by the federal government or utility companies, thereby providing a very low tax base. Twenty percent of the population is sixty and over. Of that number, twenty-three percent of the elderly are low income. Alana Minear, Director, told me about how a senior center can help the elderly. The variety of the interventions illustrate how complex the problems of the elderly are and how difficult it would be to solve these problems unaided. Alana stated that the following services have been offered:

- a medical equipment loan program for wheelchairs, etc.
- the providing of physicians for programs by the American Medical Association
- concessions from local doctors and professionals for discounts on services
- vans to transport seniors—Nursing home residents use our van to ride in the local fair. The residents' smiling, tear-stained faces make it all worth the effort.
- assisting seniors to get benefits such as food stamps, medical assistance, etc.
- working with Access West Virginia through the Department of Vocational Rehabilitation
- a list of physicians who will accept Medicare
- assisting seniors with home maintenance by providing chore maintenance
- grocery shopping, obtaining medicines, escorting, reading, writing, and interpreting correspondence for the homebound elderly
- alerting seniors to consumer protection laws and unethical salesmen—were instrumental in getting a license suspended from a questionable hearing aid salesman

- reduced admission rates for West Virginia University sports activities
- qualified professionals to speak to seniors about their concerns: funeral planning, estate planning, wills, over-the-counter drugs, dealing with death and dying, loneliness
- health screenings, blood pressure, glucose testing, hearing screening, etc.

The Independents

It is easier for elderly people to maintain hope and build upon their strengths if they have role models, whose lifestyles reflect independence. Lewis Crippen, Executive Director, told me about the Dauphin County Area Agency on Aging, Pennsylvania's program. Each year the Agency profiles fifty older people in a booklet of inspirational vignettes, to encourage all older people to help themselves to independence. Here are a few examples:

Once a construction worker, always a construction worker. Charles was a crane operator before he retired.. Today, he will stop and observe anywhere there is construction going on. Charles claims that faith can help people overcome handicaps and loneliness. His one big wish is to see peace throughout the world. He is an active member of the Congregational Evangelical Church. He volunteers his service at the Highspire Senior Center. You can always see him in his car driving people to the market, doctor's office, senior centers, etc.

"Age is a state of mind and I'm thinking young." Mrs. V. has a personal commitment to the Center City Meals on Wheels. A widow for the past twenty-four years, Mrs. V. has kept alive her independent spirit by keeping busy with activities related to helping others. For eleven years Mrs. V. has helped the Meals on Wheels program grow under her inspiring leadership. Her energies have also led her to many Hadassah positions, to being a guild member of the Jewish Home, and to become an active member of Kesher Israel Sisterhood.

Chaplain Edward W. is a widower with a large family, including one great-great grandchild. A graduate of the School of the Bible, he is no longer working, but volunteers his services. He likes to be among people, keeps active and guides others to God. Edward encourages seniors to attend church and to join senior citizen groups. He visits hospitals and homes and is currently President of the Retired Men's Club of the YMCA. Edward loves to sing. Trusting in the Lord, he strives to "Do unto others as you would have them do unto you." At age ninety-two, Chaplain Edward comes to our Center every day and offers encouragement to the other senior citizens. He gives the blessing each day, reads the Bible, leads patriotic songs and salutes the flag on a regular basis. He is living proof that a cheerful, helpful attitude shows through. His face just beams with kindness.

Doctors

Your doctor will advise you as to what level of care your elderly relative needs. Then you will have to decide if you have the resources to manage this level of care at home with the assistance of family, friends, and volunteers as needed, or if the person needs professional nursing care at home, or if a stay in a nursing home for rehabilitation is essential. Many doctors will not follow a patient who enters a nursing home a long distance away from the doctor's practice. If you are willing to drive your relative to the doctor's office, this will not present problems, unless your relative feels too ill to travel. It might be advisable to look into the possibility of changing doctors, if the nursing home is inconvenient for your doctor to visit.

If your relative is under the care of a specialist, then you have a different set of potential problems. An outstanding specialist is probably involved in teaching in a medical school, research, and writing. His office hours are from 8:30 a.m. to 10:00 a.m. on a Friday. If you are working at that time, you have to make arrangements for someone else to accompany your relative because there is no flexibility. Also, the close family doctor/patient relationship is usually not there. I recently went to a specialist for a health problem. I was worried about having a certain procedure, because of potential complications. He told me, "I have never had a patient develop complications after this procedure, but if you do, I will write you up in a research journal." The younger generation of doctors has normally been more exposed to seminars on meeting the psychosocial needs of patients.

Your doctor will probably order multiple tests before making a definite diagnosis of your elderly relative's health problem. One reason for this is that signs and symptoms are less prominent in the elderly, and may even be atypical for the medical disease that has caused them. Another reason is that people have a loophole to sue their doctors if the doctor does not order every test which might have a relationship to the patient's disease. I overheard an experienced general practitioner tell off a resident who had just ordered a complete battery of tests for a patient, in a shotgun approach. He showed the resident which tests to select for this particular health problem, and stated that if the practitioner's physical examination the next day indicated the need for further tests he would do them. The patient's condition was improving, and on her limited income she could not afford hundreds of dollars for unnecessary tests. "I am 99% sure of her diagnosis with the information I have. If complications occur, I can handle them."

"Well I want to be 100% sure." Unfortunately, medicine is an art not a science, and 100% certainty is unobtainable. In today's malpractice-oriented world, the resident's attitude is understandable.

Elderly people should be accompanied when they go for these tests. A friend described a difficult episode she encountered when taking her father-in-law for tests after his stroke. The ambulance drove them to the large teaching hospital, at a cost of $100. When they got there, they were told to go home since the test was delayed for four hours. Since they could not afford to pay an extra $200 to the ambulance firm, they waited at the hospital. Moral: call ahead and make sure the department has you scheduled and the time is right.

After the test was completed, my friend asked why her father-in-law had to wait so long lying wrapped in a blanket on a cart before being told he could go home. At last one hour after the test a staff person told her that her father-in-law's pants were lost, and he could go home when the pants were found. The old man threw off his blanket and showed that he was wearing his pants. It is difficult to comprehend how such things could happen. Tests are often essential. But they are very expensive and usually exhaust the patient. An assertive relative who asks questions is invaluable at this time, to be a friend/advocate.

Support Groups

There are many different consumer groups which were formed to give information and offer emotional support to people suffering from certain diseases. Examples would be the American Heart Association and the American Diabetes Association. A hospital usually has an acute care focus, whereas with the increase in people with chronic illnesses, we need more research and education in this area. Also, consumers are making themselves heard in many different areas of their lives. Statements made by physicians and nurses are no longer accepted without question. A rationale has to be given.

All of us have physical acute health problems or depression and stress problems at times, but the person who is having difficulty living with a chronic illness can be overwhelmed by these minor acute problems which others can handle. In a self-help group, members give advice to each other about daily living with a chronic illness. The larger organizations also have publications whose content has been checked by a physician or appropriate health worker.

The type of work done by the group will depend upon the nature of the disease process that the group is interested in. For example, ostomy groups talk about new developments in colostomy bags, diets and social relationships, while heart disease groups talk about CPR classes, but do not discuss medication dosages. I have found in my research with self-help groups that people who belong value the education, companionship, and opportunity to be of service as a volunteer to others newly diagnosed as having the particular disease. People who do not belong perceive they do not need this support, and sometimes state that they do not want to segregate themselves into an association with people who also have their chronic illness.

As with any other organization, you tend to get the regulars who attend every meeting. Other members attend sporadically, or leave after a few months. Certain people are very open about discussing their emotions and health problems—even to the point of monopolizing the conversation and boring other people. Other people are very sensitive to suggestions for change from the group.

One group member informed the group that her doctor never told her the side effects of the powerful antihypertensive medication that he ordered. His rationale was that if he told her about them, she would begin to experience the side effects. I expressed my opinion that knowing the side effects of a drug promoted safety, since you would identify the side effect sooner, and if necessary contact your doctor to change the dosages, before the drug did you serious damage. My suggestion was not accepted.

People who are regulars perceive that they are getting something from the group, and they make friends within the group. In general, regulars perceive that the group enhances their knowledge and skill in managing their chronic illness.

Suggestion

1 National Second Surgical Opinion Program Hotline (800)638-6833, (800)492-6603 in Maryland. Contact this resource as needed, for help in locating a specialist near you for a second opinion in non-emergency surgery. A service of the Health Care Financing Administration, U.S. Department of Health and Human Services.

in conclusion

This book has offered suggestions on how to promote independence in the elderly. Having read this book you should know how to:

(1) Adapt to the physiological and psychosocial changes of aging

(2) Handle stress

(3) Prevent chronic illness

(4) Maintain a healthy lifestyle

(5) Understand and cope with common chronic health problems

(6) Obtain assistance when necessary

The examples I have given will suggest other ways to maintain independence. Your local branch of the Administration on Aging will assist you in finding out about local community agencies, which have a mission to help the elderly and offer the more vigorous elderly the opportunity for volunteering and role-modeling.

Abuse of aged, 166
Accidents, 18, 26–27, 32–36
    falls, 18, 32–33
    prevention of, 32–36
Activities of Daily Living, 5, 121–122
Adaptation, 14–24, 70–76
Adult day care centers, 3, 10, 71, 144–145,
    165–166
Advocate, 98–100, 179
Aging, 3, 5, 14–24, 70–76, 177–178
    physical changes in, 5, 14–24
    psychosocial changes in, 70–76
    strengths in, 3, 177–178
Alcohol, 20, 72–73
Alzheimer's disease, 16, 163–166
Arthritis, 81, 157–158
Arts, 85–91
    music therapy, 88–89, 91
    poetry, 88
    theater, 86
Assistance from others, 173–180
    support groups, 179–180

Body temperature problems, 15–16
Brain, aging, 15, 163–165

Cancer, 148–154
    sites of cancer, 152–154
Chronic obstructive pulmonary disease,
    78–80, 145–146
    asthma, 78–80, 145

bronchitis, 146
    emphysema, 146
Communication problems, 13, 143
Community agencies, 8–13
Congestive heart failure, 141–142

Death of a spouse, 6–7
Delirium, 163–164
Dementia, 164–165
Dental problems, 16
Depression, 9, 37, 72, 164
Developmental tasks, 5–7
Diabetes, 17, 142, 158–160
Disabled, 33, 43, 124–125
Doctors, 178–179
Drugs, 20, 22, 72–73, 128–139
    dependency, 72–73
    education, 130–136
    polypharmacy, 128–130
    side effects, 20, 132–133

Education, 35–36, 65–67, 70, 86
    community, 35–36
    employment training program, 65–67
    learning, 70, 86
Elderly, see Aging
Elimination problems, 17, 124
Emergencies, 119, 140, 141, 156
Employment, 62–68
Environmental support, 14, 34–36
Equipment, adaptive, 23, 125, 158

Equipment, adaptive *(continued)*
  kitchen aids, 158
Exercise, 37–43

Family assistance, 4, 14, 23, 91
Financial, 4, 14, 55–69, 112–113
  budget, 56–57
  Medicaid, 59
  Medicare, 60–61
  insurance, 61–62
  home equity, 112–113
Foot care, 159
Forgetfulness, 163
Fractures, recurring, 156
Functional ability, 14, 124–126

Grandparenting, 96–98
Gastrointestinal problems, 160–161

Handicapped, *see* Disabled
Health screening, 12, 18–19, 25, 31–32
Hearing impairment, 21–24
Homemakers, 9
Housing, 7, 10–13, 98, 103–113
  adaptation of, 111–112
  homesharing, 104–108
  hotels, 10–13
Human needs, 9
Hypertension, 80–81, 142

Immobility, 17–18, 37–38, 123
  osteoporosis, 17–18, 37–38
  pressure sores, 17, 38
Independence, 3–14, 23, 177–178
  dependence, 4, 8
Influenza, 27
Intellect, diminished, 163–166
Intergenerational interaction, 8–9, 96–98

Kidney failure, 161

Legal aspects, 92–102
  guardianship, 92, 100–103
  protective services, 92
  wills, 92
Library services, 18, 24
  talking books, 18
Lifestyle changes, 15

Loneliness, 9

Meals-on-Wheels, 12, 48–51
Mental health, promotion, 74–76
Medication, *see* Drugs
Metabolism, impaired 16–17

Networking, 4, 10–13
Nurses, community, 27–31, 144–145,
    155–156, 174–175
Nursing care, basic, 117–127
  environmental aspects, 123
  observations, 119–121
  skills, 123–124
Nursing home, 108–111
Nutrition, 12, 17, 44–54
  budget, 47
  congregate meals, 12
  diet, balanced, 44–47, 52–53
  dieting tips, 52–54

Obesity, 44, 51
Occupational disease, 26
Occupational therapist, 125–126
Organic brain syndrome, acute,
    see Delirium
Organic brain syndrome, chronic,
    see Dementia
Oxygenation, impaired, 15

Pain, 140–141, 150, 156
Peripheral vascular disease, 140–141
Pharmacist, 129, 132
Physiotherapist, 143–145
Pneumonia, 146
Prevention of chronic illness, 4, 25–36
  levels of prevention, 26–32
Prostate gland, enlarged, 162

Rehabilitation program, 143–145
Reminiscence, 90, 126
Retirement, 6

Self-care, 8, 124–126
Senior center, 8, 10–13, 176–177
Sexuality, 73–74
Shelter, *see* Housing
Sleep, 82–83
Smoking, 15, 17, 26–27

Social isolation, 9, 75
  pet therapy, 75
Social participation, 7, 144-145
  group participation, 144-145
Social security, 11, 13
Social workers, 12, 74-76, 125-126
Stress, 26, 77-84, 125-126
  biological rhythms, 81-82
  group sessions, 125-126
  progressive muscle relaxation, 82
  transcendental meditation, 83
Stroke, 142-145

Transportation, 110-111

Urinary tract infection, 161-162

Vision impairment, 14, 18-21, 24, 35-36
  blindness, 20-21, 24, 35-36
  cataracts, 18-19
  driving tips, 19-20, 36
  glaucoma, 19
Volunteers, 10, 35-36, 64-65, 96,
    131-134, 167-172
  elderly, 96, 167-172
  ministry, 35-36, 64-65, 131-134
  retired health professionals, 10

Wellness assessment, 27-31

RANDALL LIBRARY-UNCW

3 0490 0334809 0